IMAGES
of America
EARLY ABILENE

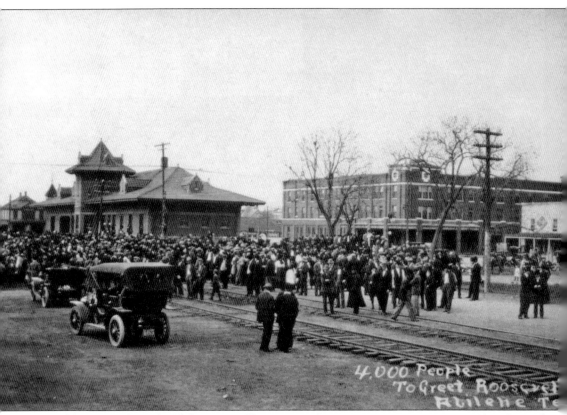

Teddy Roosevelt made Abilene one of his stops on his cross-country train trip in 1911. Several hundred citizens turned out to see and hear Roosevelt speak at the train depot when his train stopped for a brief period.

ON THE COVER: Chief J. J. Clinton poses in his office in early Abilene. Chief Clinton was an Indian scout and lawman in Kansas before coming to Abilene where he was fire chief and chief of police for over 30 years.

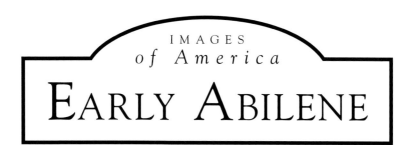
IMAGES of America
EARLY ABILENE

Jack E. North

Copyright © 2010 by Jack E. North
ISBN 978-0-7385-7954-2

Published by Arcadia Publishing
Charleston, South Carolina

Printed in the United States of America

Library of Congress Control Number: 2010932242

For all general information, please contact Arcadia Publishing:
Telephone 843-853-2070
Fax 843-853-0044
E-mail sales@arcadiapublishing.com
For customer service and orders:
Toll-Free 1-888-313-2665

Visit us on the Internet at www.arcadiapublishing.com

*I dedicate this book to all the families that have
shared their memories of Abilene's history.*

Contents

Acknowledgments		6
Introduction		7
1.	Abilene Pioneers	9
2.	Early Abilene Businesses	31
3.	Entertainment in Early Abilene	107
4.	Early Abilene Churches and Schools	115

Acknowledgments

The families of Abilene pioneers have shared the majority of the pictures included in this book. It has been their intent to share the history of Abilene with others so that future generations will know how Abilene came about. My collection was started in 1968 and has grown to 4,000 images. It is impossible to include all the images here, but it is my intent to show a representative overall view of the pictures that were collected. Unless otherwise noted, images are courtesy of the author.

Many of the pioneers who have shared their stories have since passed on, but their stories remain, for which we will be forever grateful. There are other books available on and about Abilene, which can be found in the city library.

Introduction

This book shows readers, through pictures, the very early days of Abilene, Texas, from 1881 up to the 1930s. The Texas Legislature formed Taylor County in 1858. It was named for the Taylor brothers who were killed at the Alamo. Buffalo Gap, south of Abilene, was founded in 1878. The community grew from a handful of buffalo hunters who made their camp there because the buffaloes migrated through a natural gap in the Callahan Divide, which was a range of mesas south of Abilene.

By the 1870s, soldiers and Texas Rangers had mainly driven the Native Americans out of this part of the state. The buffalo herds that once roamed the prairies had disappeared due to their slaughtering. These grasslands were a natural place for the ranchers that followed.

The Texas and Pacific Railroad was making its way from Fort Worth, Texas, in 1881. Due to two different surveys of Taylor County, there was a legal cloud over the land titles around the Buffalo Gap community, which had been named the county seat in 1878. This was one of the main reasons the train line decided to extend their tracks through the northern part of Taylor County instead of through Buffalo Gap. At a meeting at the Hashknife ranch, interested parties decided to form a new town, which the train line referred to as "The Future Great." Col. C. W. Merchant, a local rancher, was given the task of naming the new town. Abilene was chosen because they wanted it to become a major cattle-shipping point like Abilene, Kansas.

The official town lot sale was on March 15, 1881. Business lots went for $100 to $250, and residential lots went for $100. It took two days to sell all of the lots, which were held in very muddy conditions. Soon, Abilene took on all the aspects of a Wild West town. People came from many states to settle it. In 1883, a county-wide vote, which was eventually settled by the county commissioners, moved the county seat to Abilene. In 1884, a new county courthouse was started, and Abilene was growing. Merchants, saloons, and churches were soon opened. In 1902, Abilene was voted dry, and the town settled down.

All the pioneers cannot be included in this book, but they are given a strong representation. Churches, colleges, and early businesses are included. The military played a very important part of Abilene's later history, but that is another story in itself. Camp Barkeley and Dyess Air Force Base have been major factors in Abilene's economy since World War II.

So pull up an easy chair and learn about Abilene, Texas, first called "The Future Great."

One
ABILENE PIONEERS

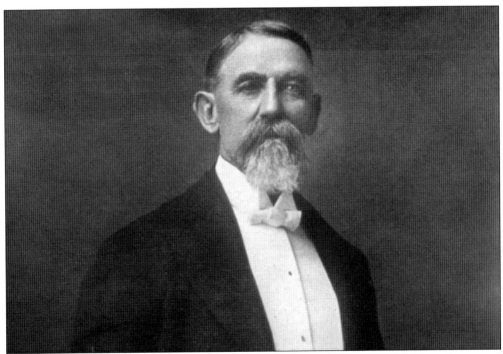

C. W. Merchant, a rancher, named the city of Abilene after Abilene, Kansas, because he wanted it to become a major shipping station for cattle. Born on August 31, 1836, Merchant came to the Abilene area in 1874 and built the first stone house there in 1881. He served as a bank president and was very active in the growth of the town. Abilene mourned the death of Merchant, its last founding father, in 1926. (Courtesy of the Merchant family.)

James Harrison Parramore, a rancher and founding father of Abilene, was born on August 13, 1840, in Early County, Georgia. He served with Terry's Texas Rangers in the Civil War and moved to Abilene in 1881. He became partners with C. W. Merchant in the cattle business. They operated several ranches including the San Simon, a large ranch in Arizona. He was one of the largest cattle raisers in the state for many years. Parramore had a belief in higher education and was a founding benefactor of the West Texas Baptist College, which is now Hardin-Simmons University in Abilene. His family lived at 710 Orange Street in Abilene, which was a modern home in 1881. Abilene named a street in his honor. The entire block where the home was located is maintained today, even though the home is not there. Abilene lost this founding father in 1917. (Courtesy of the Parramore family.)

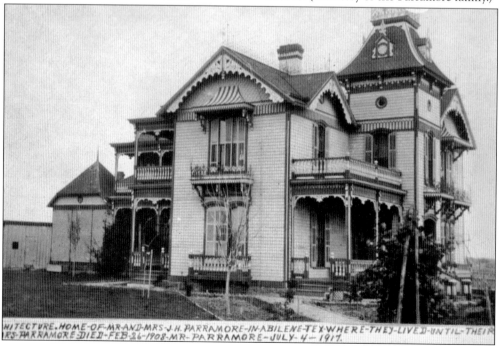

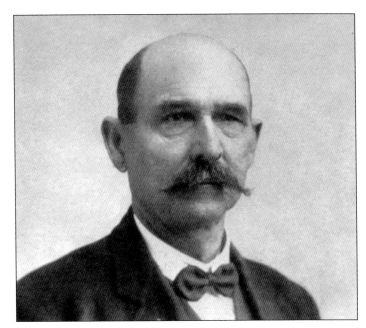

John Cunningham was a pioneer, Indian fighter, and sheriff of Taylor County. Born on February 14, 1846, in Comanche, Texas, Cunningham moved to Buffalo Gap, Texas, as a young man. He served under the command of his father in the Texas Rangers. When he married, he and his wife moved to Abilene in 1881, and he became one of the best-known peacemakers by serving as sheriff of Taylor County for 25 years. Death claimed this lawmaker in 1925. (Courtesy of the Cunningham family.)

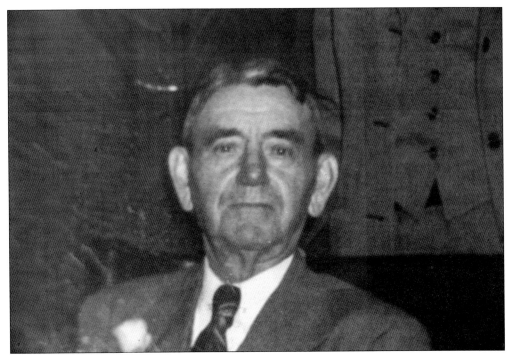

John Thomas Leeson Sr. was a pioneer Abilene grocer. He was born April 23, 1870, in Dubuque, Iowa. Leeson moved to Abilene in 1882 with his parents and went to work in a grocery store at age 14. He opened his own store at North Second and Pine Streets in 1896. He was known to carry families for a year before they could pay him. Leeson delivered orders to homes in his horse-drawn wagon. He died in 1960. (Courtesy of the Leeson family.)

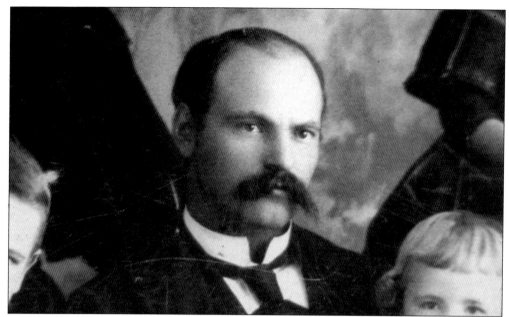

David S. Kauffman was a pioneer saddle maker in Abilene. He was born March 20, 1862, in Pennsylvania. Kauffman moved to Abilene in the 1880s to join his brother Pete in the saddlery business. His family attended the First Baptist church and was baptized in Lytle Creek. The family lived on Victoria Street where they reared six children. The Kauffman Brothers Saddlery was located in the 200 block of Pine Street where they sold handmade saddles and other products related to the leather business. Their best handmade saddle sold for $35 in 1905. He also farmed near Nugent, north of Abilene, but returned to Abilene where they lived at South Second and Elm Streets. Kauffman died in 1935. (Courtesy of the Kauffman family.)

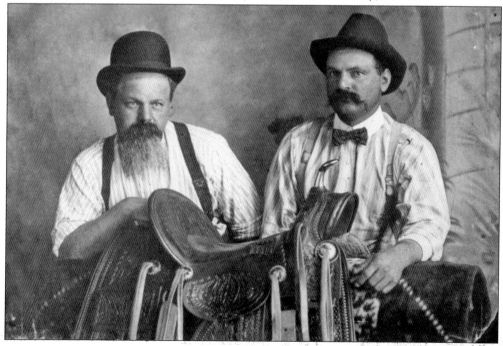

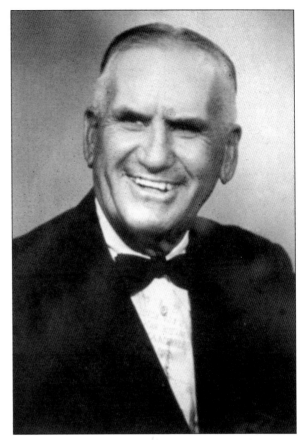

Sheriff Will Watson was born on September 7, 1884, in Abilene at 342 Poplar Street where he lived all his life. From delivering newspapers to a world-known personality, Watson rode horseback with the Hardin-Simmons College band for 35 years. He traveled the world with them. Watson and his horse Silver were the first horse and rider to walk up the steps of the U.S. Capitol in Washington, D.C. The 1950 West Texas Fair was dedicated to him for his over 50 years of working with the fair. Gov. Price Daniel commissioned him Ambassador of Good Will of Texas in 1957. His large Western hat, six-shooters, and his white outfit were known the world over. Death claimed this showman in 1963.

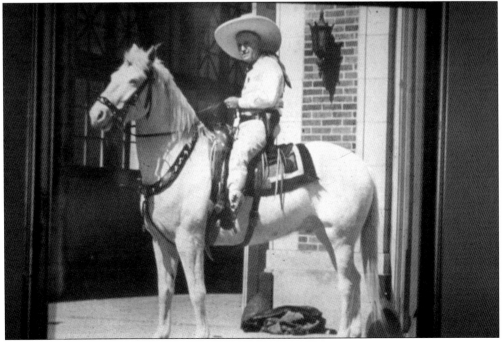

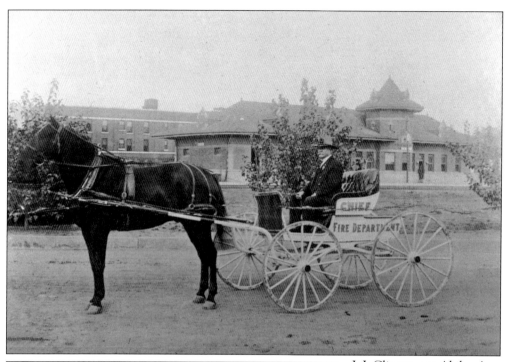

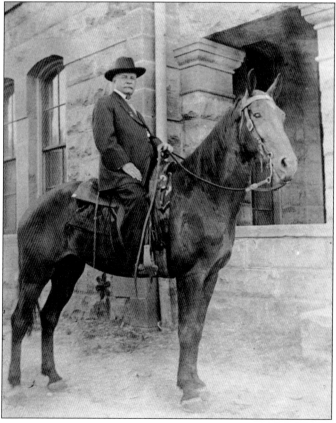

J. J. Clinton was Abilene's pioneer fire and police chief. Born in 1848 in Ireland, young Clinton came to the United States to start an exciting and varied career. After serving in the Confederate army, he became an Indian scout for the army in Texas. He traveled over the site of Abilene in 1867 on the way to Dodge City, Kansas, where he served as city marshal. He settled in Abilene in 1884 where he became fire and police chief at the same time. This peaceful man, who had notches on his gun, kept the peace in Abilene for 38 years. He is remembered for his custom of firing his gun at South First and Chestnut Streets at midnight on New Year's Eve as a signal for the saloons to close. Abilene mourned the death of the peacemaker in 1922.

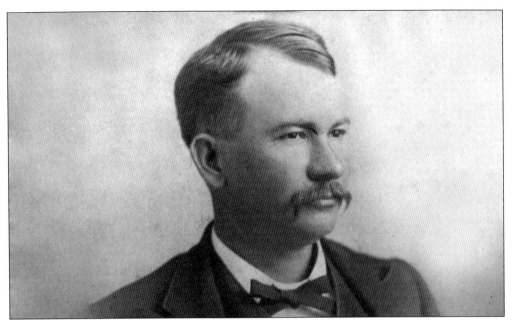

T. M. Willis was a pioneer lawyer and judge in Abilene. He was born on June 27, 1859, in Georgia. Willis moved to Texas as a young boy and graduated from Cumberland University with a degree in law in 1883. He moved to Abilene in 1881, where he practiced law. The voters of Abilene elected him city judge in 1921. Death claimed this pioneer lawyer in 1937. (Courtesy of the Willis family.)

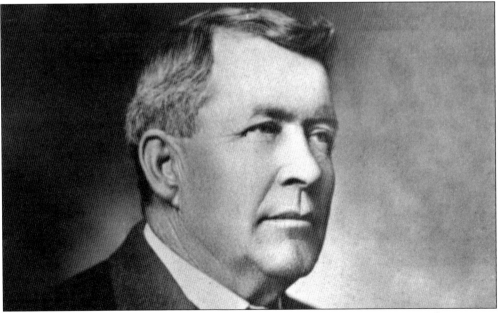

J. P. Wooten was a horse trader and wholesaler in early Abilene. Born in 1855 in Cophia County, Mississippi, Wooten moved to Abilene in 1886 from Central America. From his livery and stable business, he became known as a good horse trader. He also operated a stage line to Ballinger, Texas. Wooten served Abilene as its police and health commissioner for many years before his death in 1928. (Courtesy of the Wooten family.)

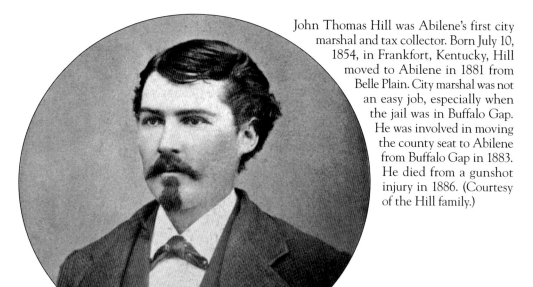

John Thomas Hill was Abilene's first city marshal and tax collector. Born July 10, 1854, in Frankfort, Kentucky, Hill moved to Abilene in 1881 from Belle Plain. City marshal was not an easy job, especially when the jail was in Buffalo Gap. He was involved in moving the county seat to Abilene from Buffalo Gap in 1883. He died from a gunshot injury in 1886. (Courtesy of the Hill family.)

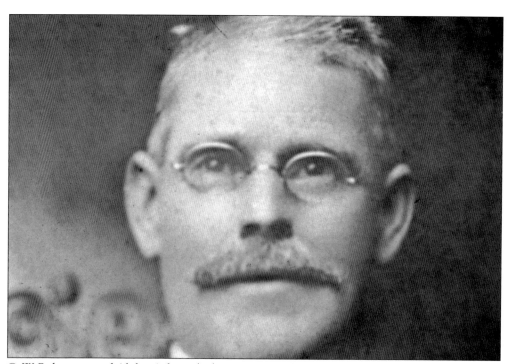

C. W. Roberts owned Abilene's first telephone company. Born May 17, 1852, in Tennessee, Roberts moved to Abilene in 1885 from Rusk, Texas, where he started the Abilene Telephone Company that same year. He ran telephone lines, which included tie-ins to barb wire, to Merkel and Anson in 1897. He was an accountant until his death in 1926. (Courtesy of the Roberts family.)

Robert H. Parker was born September 16, 1828, in Kentucky and served in the Confederate army before moving to Abilene in 1883. He owned the Parker Lumber Company and built the first two-story home in Abilene. He was active in the Presbyterian Church. Parker and his wife raised 10 children at their home at South Second and Butternut Streets. This active businessman died in 1896. (Courtesy of the Parker family.)

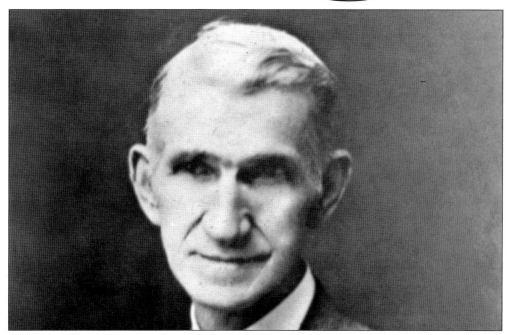

Henry A. Tillet Sr. was born May 23, 1860, in Hendersonville, North Carolina, and moved to Abilene in 1883, where he was a land lawyer and owner of an abstract company. He was Abilene's first school superintendent and served as a state senator. This pioneer died in 1930. (Courtesy of the Tillet family.)

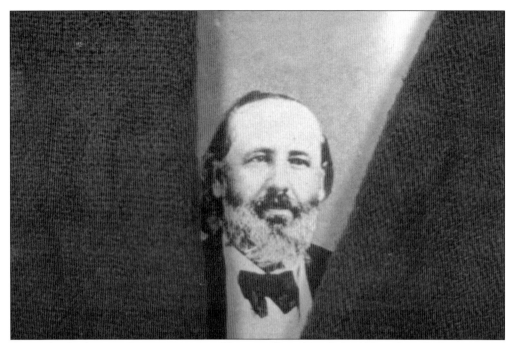

Gen. John Sayles was a lawyer, writer, and lecturer. Born March 9, 1825, in Oneida County, New York, he was admitted to the State Bar of Texas in 1846. He served as adjutant general under General Magruder during the Civil War. He practiced law and wrote law books in Washington County for over 40 years where he attained high standing in the legal profession. Sayles helped start Baylor Law School. The family moved to Abilene in 1886 and helped start Simmons College in 1891. He was the first Texas writer of legal treatises, including *Masonic Jurisprudence*. He was also the first of several generations of lawyers in his family. Sayles died in 1897. (Courtesy of the Sayles family.)

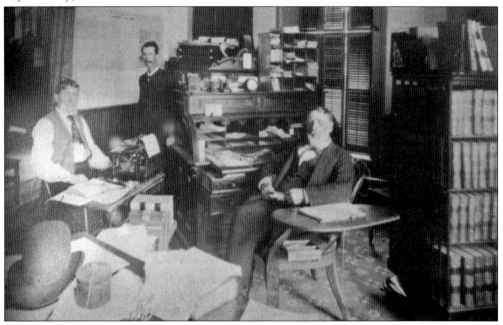

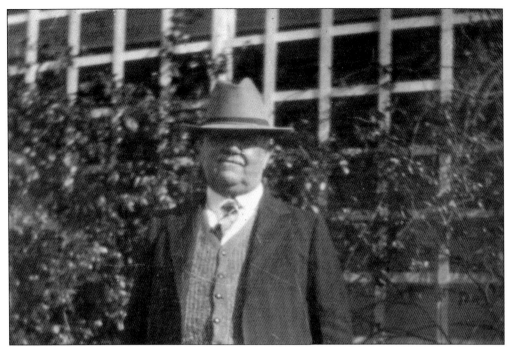

C. C. Tate was born April 24, 1864, and was a pioneer dry goods businessman. He moved to Abilene in 1891 and operated the Tate Dry Goods Store at South First and Chestnut Streets. His family members were charter members of St. Paul Methodist Church and his daughter Jenny was the first head of the math department at McMurry College. This pioneer died in 1937. (Courtesy of the Tate family.)

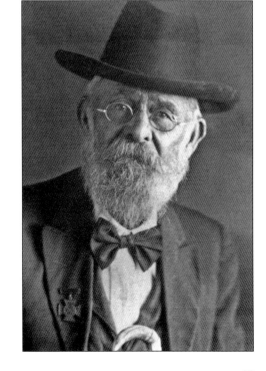

Jabus Booker Greenway was born February 25, 1837, in Polk County, North Carolina. He served in the Confederate army where he was taken prisoner three different times. His family moved to Abilene in 1889. He was a prominent farmer in this area for several years. Greenway died in 1922 in Hamlin, Texas. (Courtesy of the Greenway family.)

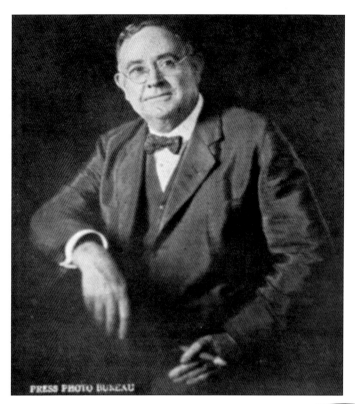

George Lee Paxton Sr. was born October 16, 1865, in Mercer County, Kentucky. He moved to Abilene in 1889 with $13 in his pocket. He went to work in a hardware store and bought it in four years. In 1907, he was made president of Citizens National Bank. Paxton continued to be very prominent in Abilene affairs until his death in 1935. (Courtesy of Paxton family.)

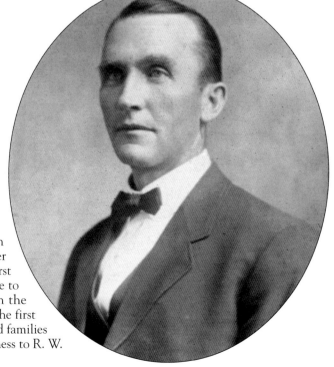

Dan. T. Laughter was born in Eudora, Mississippi, in October 1871. Laughter was Abilene's first licensed mortician, having come to Abilene in 1900. He started in the furniture business and opened the first funeral home in 1905. He served families faithfully until he sold the business to R. W. North in 1945. He died in 1952.

Dr. W. C. Fisher was a pioneer jeweler and optometrist. Born October 28, 1869, at Wills Point, Texas, Dr. Fisher sailed around the world three times as a cabin boy. He brought his family to Abilene in 1906 in one of the first automobiles that the town ever saw. In 1908, he opened the Fisher Jewelry Company at North First and Pine Streets. He moved the store three times, enlarging it every time. He received his optometry license in 1922 and added the optometrist office to his ventures. He was prominent in Abilene affairs for many years until his death in 1945. (Courtesy of the Fisher family.)

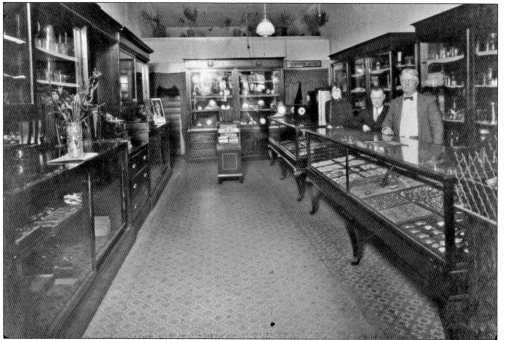

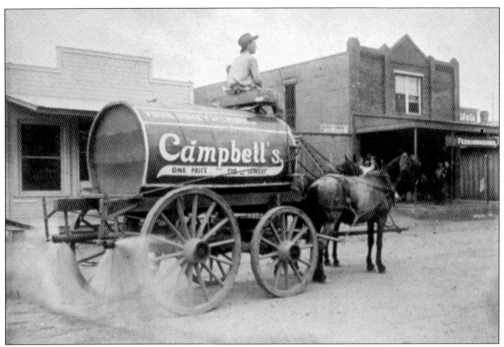

J. D. Moore was born on June 19, 1880, in Cookville, Tennessee. In the early 1900s he came to Abilene, where he started in the freight business by hauling cowhides and bones to the railroad depot by horse and wagon. He expanded his business by hauling general supplies, watering the streets to keep the dust down, and by taking large hauling jobs like moving the main beam that went into the new Abilene High School. He added the first stake body truck in Abilene. His family continued in the moving and storage business after his death in 1954.

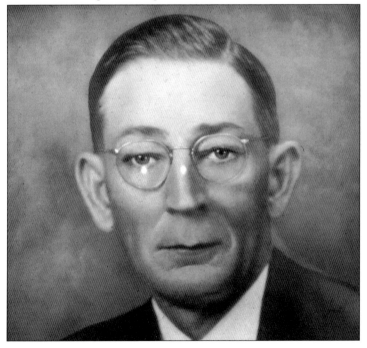

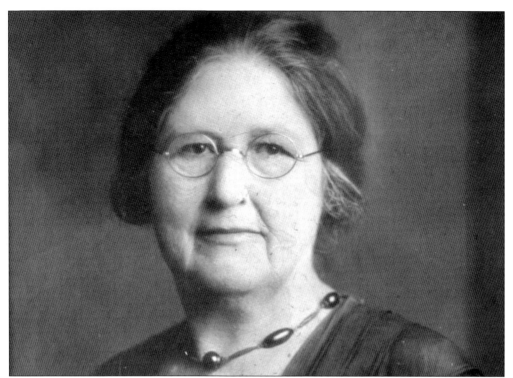

Ida B. Powers was born in Appanoose County, Iowa, on April 14, 1861. After her husband was accidently killed in 1895, she moved to Abilene to support her nine children in 1907. She worked hard long hours to make sure her children received a better education than she had. She boarded students from the Childer's Classical Institute for many years. She was the classical example of a pioneer woman until her death in 1948. (Courtesy of Powers family.)

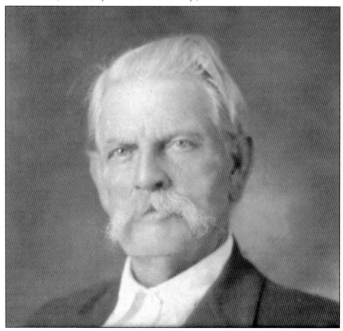

Sylvester Peter Moore was a pioneer merchant and a descendant of Sir Thomas Moore, the chancellor of England. He was born in Perryville, Missouri, on December 10, 1849, and moved to Brady, Merkel, and finally Abilene in 1908. Moore operated the Moore Dry Goods Store in the second block of Pine Street for several years. He died in 1937. (Courtesy of the Moore family.)

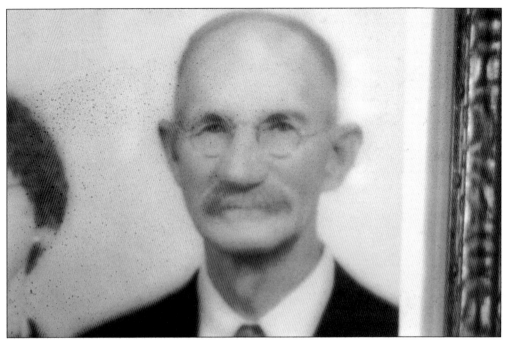

Jim Eplen was an early day merchant and cattle buyer in Abilene. Born January 17, 1872, in Milam County, Texas, Eplen came to Abilene in 1908 in an immigrant railcar. He was a partner in the Bertrand Brothers and Eplen Meat Market on Pine Street. Jim would buy cattle and drive them himself to their market. His sons Tom, Leroy, and Mack would later play major roles in Abilene. He would always help other cattlemen with their herds anytime they asked, including his friend and founder of Abilene, C. W. Merchant. This well-known cattleman died in 1946. (Courtesy of the Eplen family.)

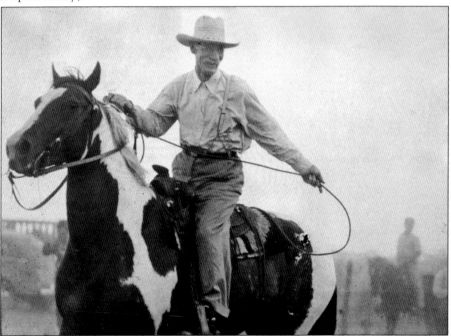

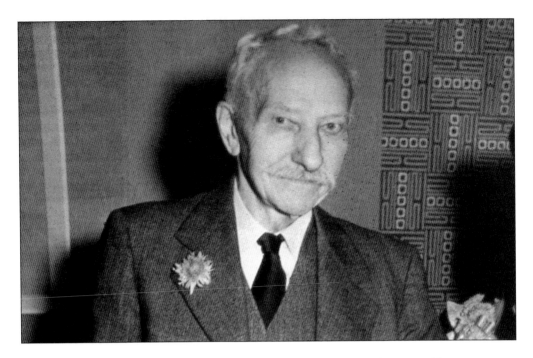

Joseph Joeris was born in Heinsberg, Germany, on February 27, 1875. He came to Texas as a young boy and went to work in a blacksmith shop in Abilene in 1889. Joeris bought the business and his brother Pete joined him there shortly after at 140 Sycamore Street. They became masters of their trade, working mainly on wagons and buggies in the early days. They shod their last horse in 1916 when the automobiles took over. They never used a tape measure, and they could look at what was broken and fix it. Death claimed this pioneer blacksmith in 1960. (Courtesy of the Joeris family.)

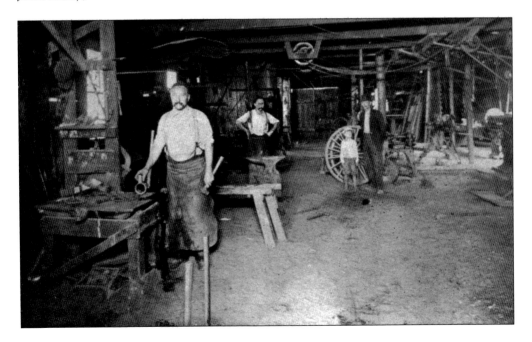

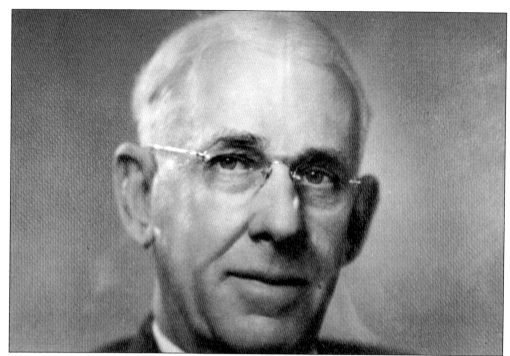

Dr. Jim Alexander was a pioneer doctor and rancher. Born in Tennessee on September 18, 1867, Dr. Jim came to Abilene in 1889 at age 22. His first office was above the Linda Theater, and in 1904, he opened the Alexander Sanitarium, which was the first hospital between Fort Worth and El Paso. In 1918, he opened the new Alexander Sanitarium on North Sixth Street where he delivered more than 2,000 babies in his 60-year career. With his sons, he accumulated large ranching holdings in the Abilene area. Abilene lost a legend when Dr. Jim died in 1954. (Courtesy of Alexander family.)

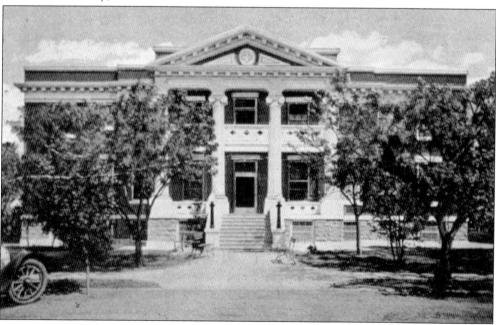

Judge E. N. Kirby was a pioneer attorney and mayor. Born November 19, 1865, in La Grange, Georgia, he came to Abilene in 1892 where he was a partner in Kirby, Kirby, and Leggett law firm. He served as mayor of Abilene for 13 years, a record that still stands. In his honor, Kirby Lake was named, and Kirby Park, which the family donated to the city, was also dedicated to him. Judge Kirby practiced law in Abilene for over 55 years. His friends would often visit him at his office and talk about their hunting trips. His annual gift of Christmas fruit to courthouse employees was long remembered after his death in 1949. (Courtesy of the Kirby family.)

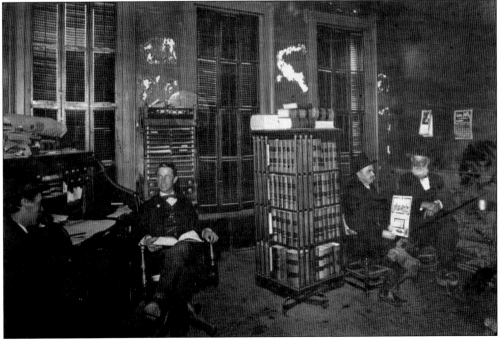

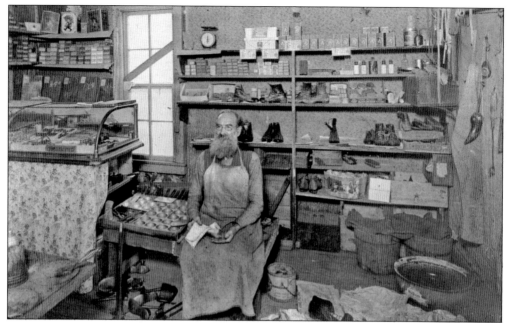

W. B. Dill was one of Abilene's shoe repair shop owners. Born March 15, 1849, in Johnstown, Pennsylvania, Dill moved to Abilene in 1892 after his wife died in Missouri. He lived at and operated his shoe repair business at North Fifth and Pine Streets. He died in 1927. (Courtesy of the Dill family.)

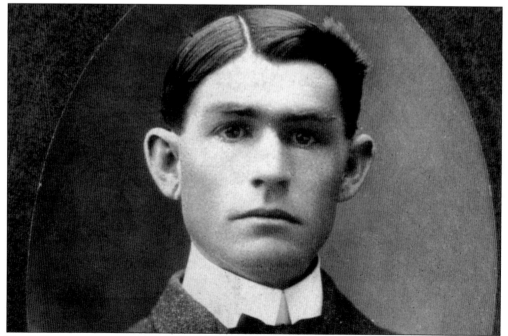

Ben L. Peevey was a pioneer lawman in Abilene. Born February 21, 1879, Peevey moved to Abilene in 1897 where he joined the Abilene Police Department and served under J. J. Clinton. In 1916, he opened a general store at Caps but later returned to the sheriff's department. Peevey died in 1956. (Courtesy of the Peevey family.)

Dallas Scarborough was Abilene's prominent trial lawyer. Born March 14, 1882, in Bushy Creek, Texas, Scarborough moved to Abilene in 1905 to attend school. After completing law school at the University of Texas, he returned to Abilene where his reputation grew as a criminal lawyer. He also served as mayor for two terms. Death claimed this pioneer in 1957. (Courtesy of the Scarborough family.)

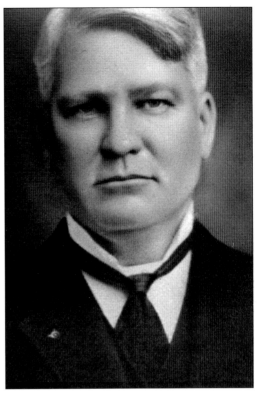

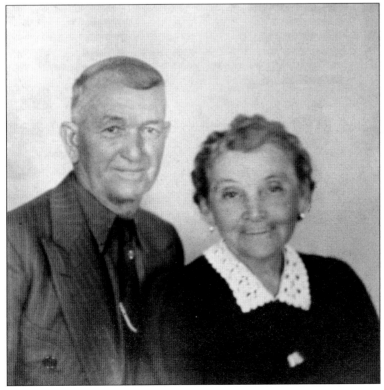

William Oscar Hampton was a pioneer restaurant owner in Abilene. Born June 12, 1881, in Collin County, Texas, Hampton moved his family to Hamby near Abilene in 1902. In 1923, his family moved into Abilene and operated the Hampton Café on North Third near the post office. W. O. Hampton died in 1942.

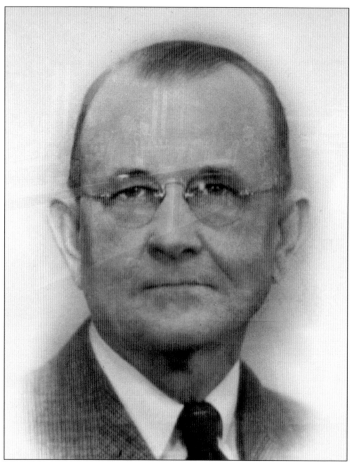

Dr. Jack M. Estes was a pioneer physician in Abilene. Born August 17, 1873, in Collin County, Texas, Dr. Jack played football on Simmons College's first football team in 1894. After getting his medical degree, he returned to Clyde, Texas, where he was the town's first doctor. He traveled many miles in his horse and buggy to see his patients. He was closely associated with Hardin-Simmons College. Dr. Jack was chief of staff at Hendricks Memorial Hospital in Abilene when he was killed in an automobile accident in California in 1937. Abilene and the Texas Legislature mourned the death of this well-known physician. (Courtesy of the Estes family.)

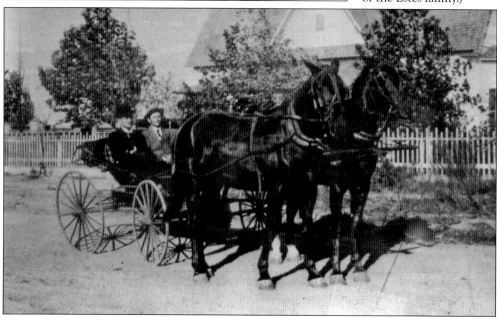

Two

EARLY ABILENE BUSINESSES

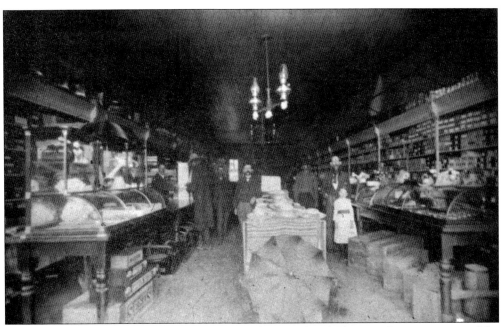

The Clayton General Merchandise Store at South Second and Chestnut Streets was one of the earliest stores in Abilene. G. W. Clayton operated several businesses including this establishment. Note the oil-burning lamp and the simple methods of displaying their goods. (Courtesy of Clayton family.)

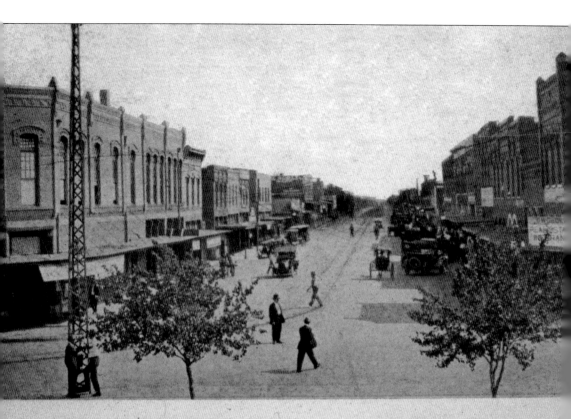

Chestnut Street scene looking south.

Chestnut Street was one of the first busy streets in early Abilene. Many of the first businesses were built on the south side of the train tracks, which ran through the middle of town east to west. Due to early fires in the downtown area, the business district shifted between the north side and the south side of the railroad tracks.

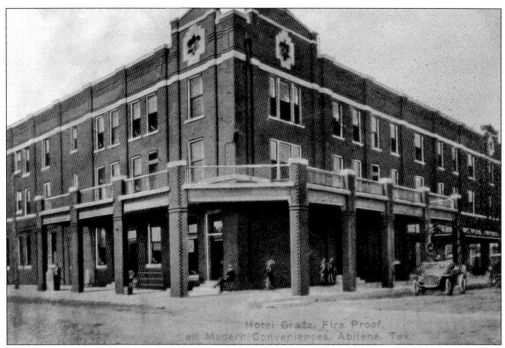

The Grace Hotel was one of the most well-constructed hotels in the downtown area. It was built at North First and Cypress Streets where it still stands today. It was called the Drake Hotel for a period, but when it was restored, the name was changed back to the Grace. Today it is called the Grace Museum and is a valuable asset to the citizens of Abilene.

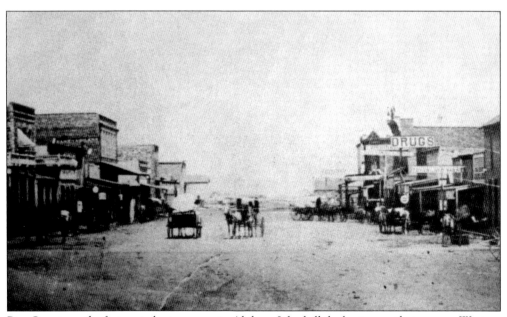

Pine Street was the first main business area in Abilene. It had all the businesses that a young Western town had: general stores, saloons, saddle and leather goods stores, dry goods, and barbershops, just to name a few. If early Abilene had it, one could find it on Pine Street.

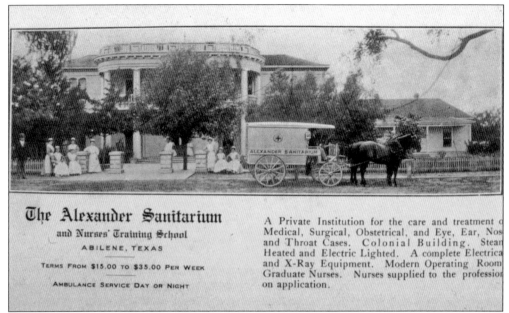

The Alexander Sanitarium was the first hospital between Fort Worth and El Paso. Rooms were $15 to $35 a week, and it housed a training school for nurses. The hospital had horse-drawn ambulances, which ran day or night. The sanitarium served Abilene well for several years. (Courtesy of the Alexander family.)

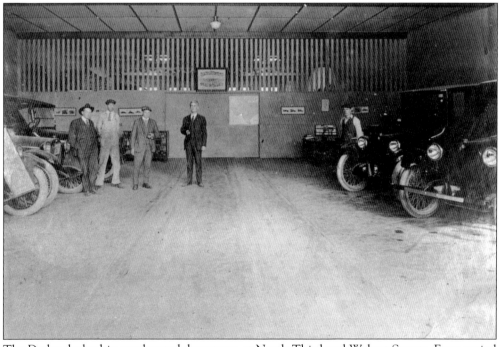

The Dodge dealership was located downtown at North Third and Walnut Streets. For a period of time, several dealerships were located downtown near the post office.

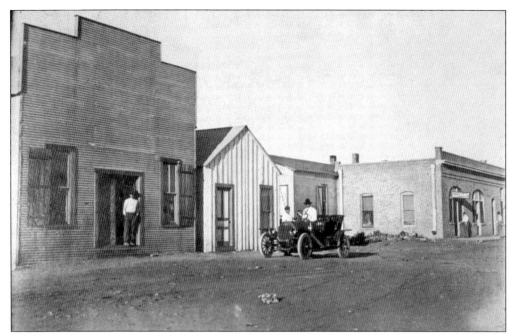

This early street scene was typical of early Abilene. Many businesses did not put up signs. This is a picture of one of the early automobiles in Abilene on an unpaved street. The city did not start paving downtown streets until 1911.

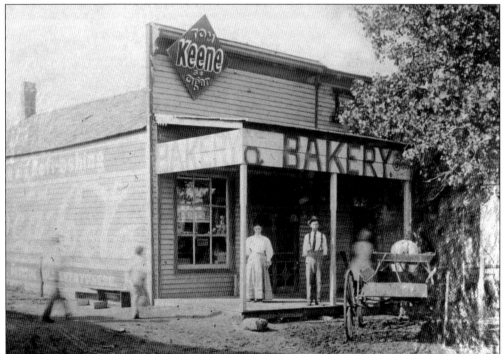

The Schultz Bakery was Abilene's first bakery. It was founded by Hermann Schultz, a German immigrant who came to the town with a German wagon train in 1878 and settled near where the town would be. When Abilene was founded, he opened the first bakery.

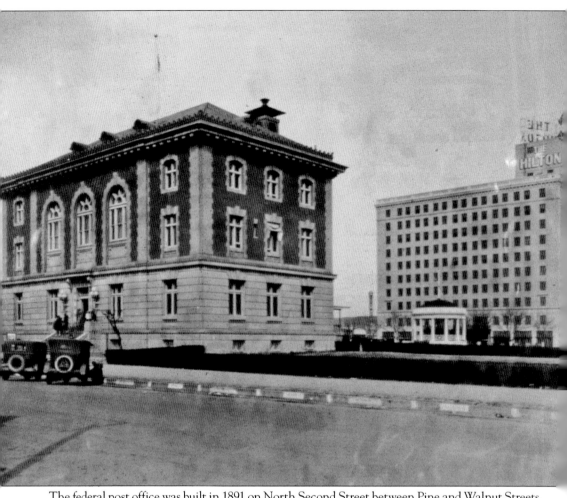

The federal post office was built in 1891 on North Second Street between Pine and Walnut Streets. The federal courtroom was on the second floor. Behind the post office was the town bandstand where large gatherings took place. Churches, bands, and speakers had meetings there. Behind the bandstand is the first hotel ever called the Hilton. Later the hotel was called the Windsor.

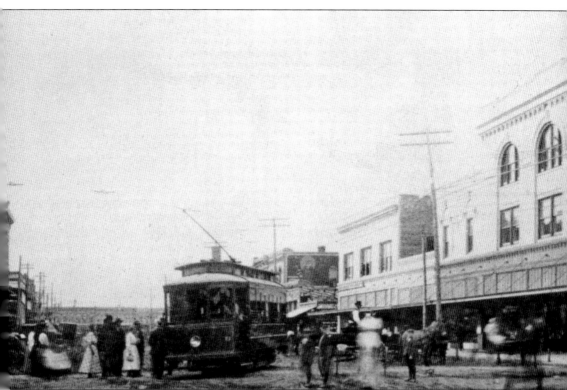

This is Pine Street in 1906. Streetcars served Abilene from 1904 until the early 1930s. People were still coming to downtown in their horse-drawn wagons to do their shopping. With the advent of the streetcar, people adjusted to more modern means of getting around town. The streets did not see paving until 1911, and only some of the main streets were paved. People enjoyed visiting with their neighbors while riding the streetcars.

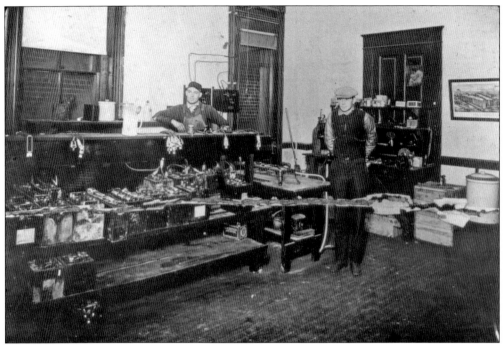

Exide Battery Company was one of the first battery companies in Abilene. It was located at South Fourth and Chestnut Streets where Nichols Battery Company is located today. A battery shop was new to the Abilene business scene at the time because of the newfound use of the automobile in everyday life.

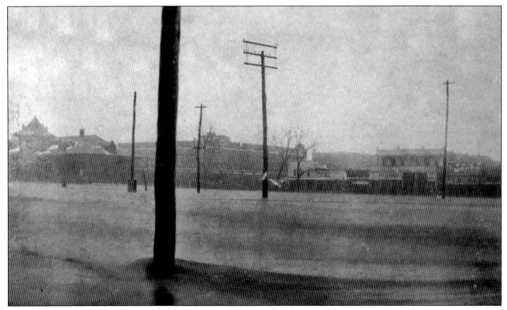

The 1911 flood and storm damage almost destroyed the business district in Abilene. The entire downtown was underwater for several days and shut down all the businesses. It took a massive cleanup effort by all of Abilene to get things back to normal.

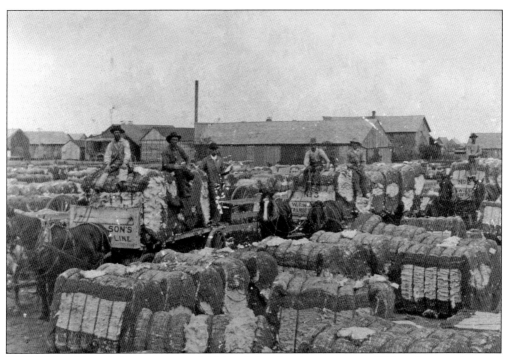

W. T. Wilson Transfer Line was one of Abilene's first freight companies. Wilson foresaw the need for a moving and storage company in the 1880s. His wagons and employees are pictured moving bales of cotton from the gins to the storage areas. His company branched out to haul water and other materials for the city and private individuals. His businesses fulfilled a need for Abilene in the early days.

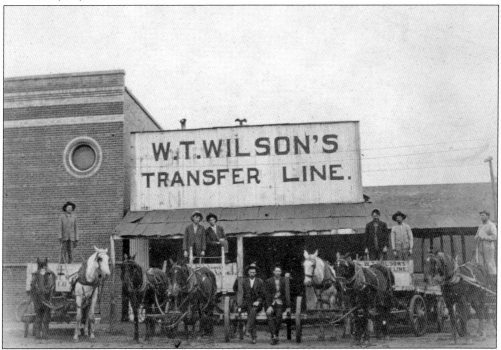

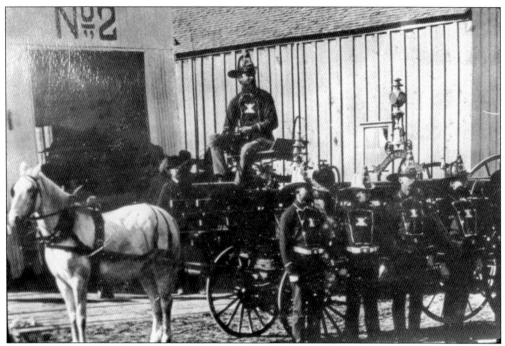

Volunteers in early Abilene manned Fire Station No. 2. A town of mainly wood buildings saw many fires that completely destroyed many of the early buildings because water was not readily available.

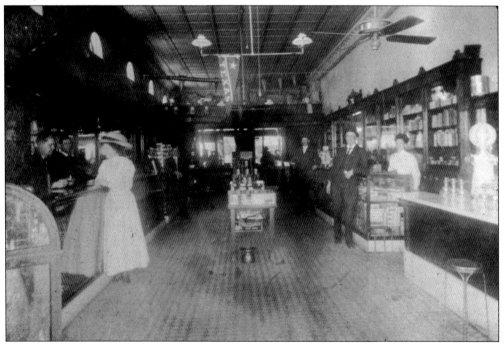

McGee's Drugstore was a popular place in early Abilene. Dr. McGee opened his drugstore in addition to his medical practice. It was quite a fancy store for its time. It was a nice place to visit with friends and neighbors.

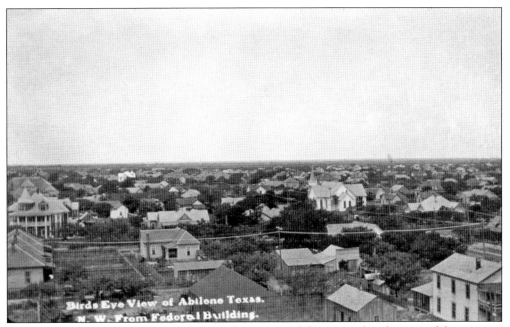

This view from the Federal Building shows downtown Abilene just after the turn of the century. The picture shows how Abilene was developed by the early 1900s. The view is looking northwest from the federal post office on North Second Street.

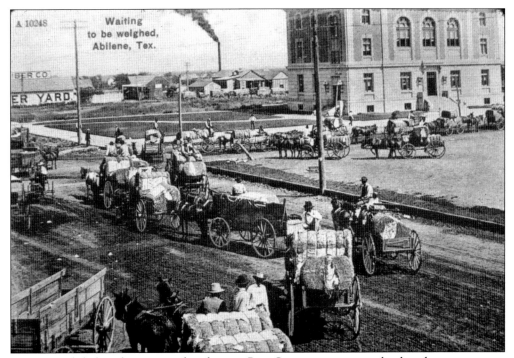

Wagons with bales of cotton are lined up on Pine Street waiting to unload at the storage area. Cotton was one of the major crops around Abilene because of the climate and rainfall.

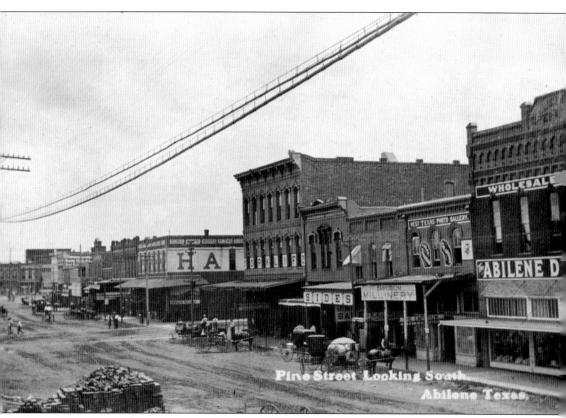

Pine Street was the main street in Abilene where most of the early businesses were located. The businesses were centrally located for their customers. There were wagon yards in the same area for citizens to park their wagons either before or after taking care of their business downtown. Most of the needs of the people could be fulfilled on Pine Street.

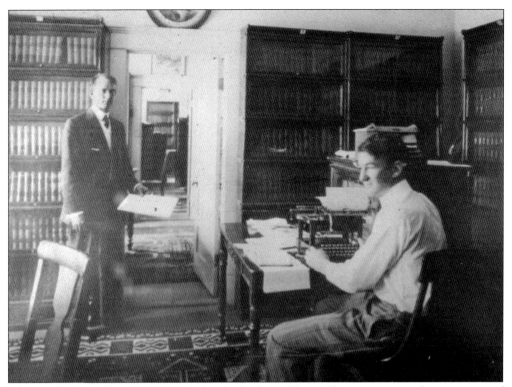

John Sayles law office was typical of early day law offices. There were several generations of the Sayles family that carried on the law practice in Abilene. Lawyers were needed in early day Abilene just as much as they are needed today. Law office libraries were kept up to date with the current books, but not all lawyers had libraries so they shared with fellow coworkers. (Courtesy of the Sayles family.)

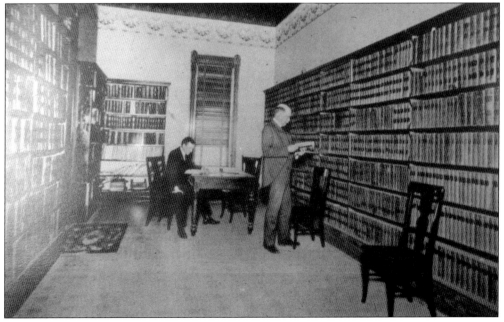

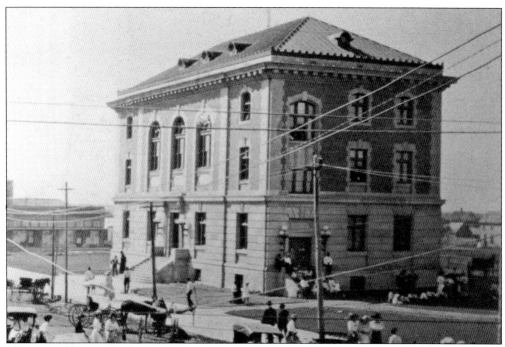
The post office was built in 1891 on North Third Street between Pine and Walnut Streets. In this picture, there was some kind of gathering around the post office. Note the transmissions lines that are in the picture.

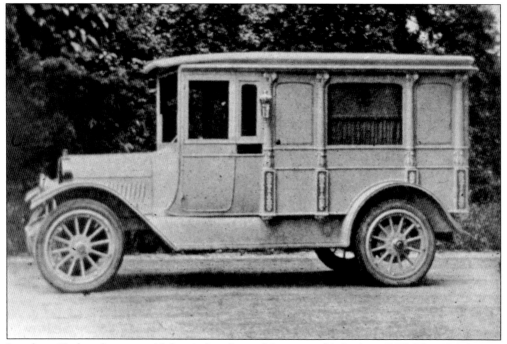
Laughter Undertaking was Abilene's first funeral home established in 1905. The 1917 hearse was one of the first motorized hearses in West Texas. Because of its size, it was also used as an ambulance in early day Abilene. (Courtesy of the Laughter family.)

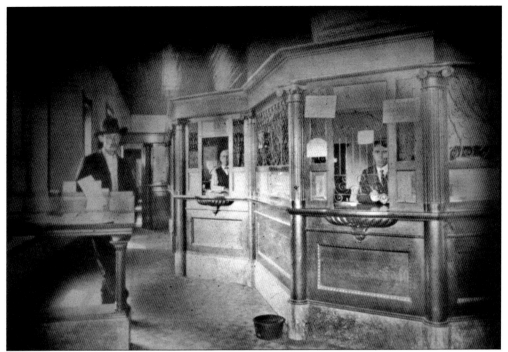

The Citizens National Bank was one of the early banks in Abilene. It was located at North First and Pine Streets. This picture shows what the original lobby looked like before 1900. Banks were another necessity in early Western towns.

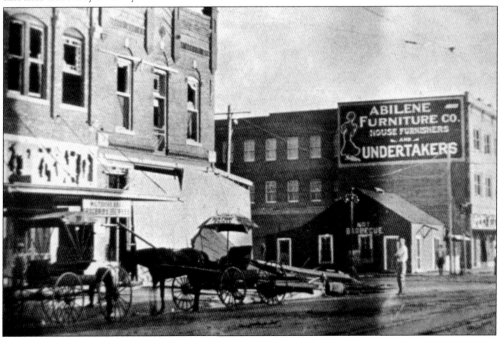

This picture of South First Street was taken after a bad storm that damaged a major portion of the city. Streetcar tracks are pictured. Notice the large advertisement for Abilene Furniture Company behind a restaurant that apparently served "hot barbecue."

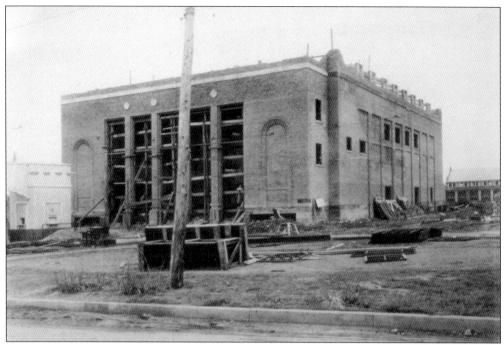

This picture shows the building of the Abilene City Auditorium on South Seventh Street near Fair Park. The auditorium was well used over the years for city and civic events. The building was constructed well and lasted many years.

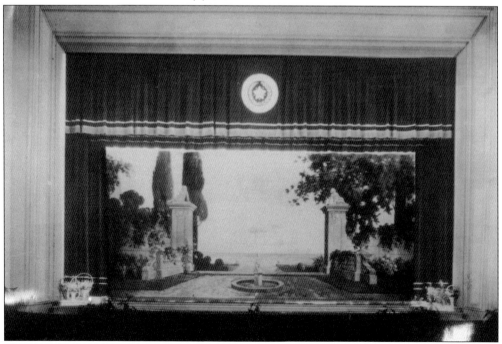

The stage at the Abilene City Auditorium drew crowds to see various productions and plays. In addition, conventions met there, wrestling matches were popular, bands performed concerts on the stage, and political rallies were held there.

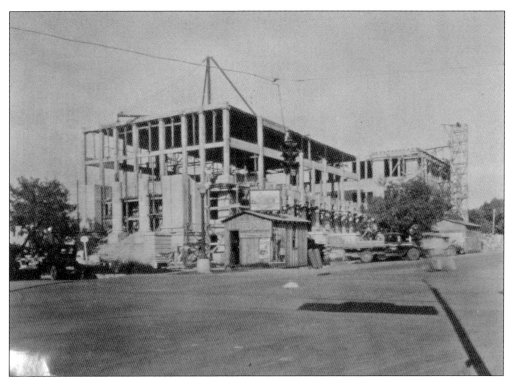

The next generation of Abilene's city hall was built on the corner of North Second and Cedar Streets. The elegant building housed the city offices in the upper floors, and the police station and jail were housed in the basement. It was erected across the street from the city library.

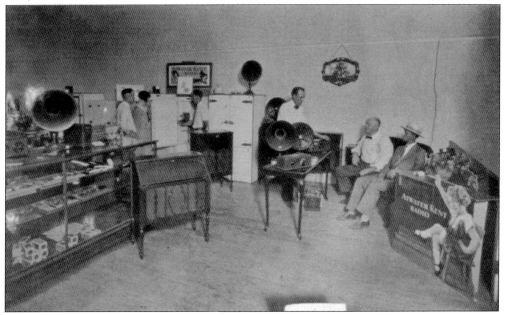

Lion Hardware was one of the first complete hardware stores in Abilene. This picture shows the electronics section of the store. Note the early radios and record players. The store played an important role in the city's early commerce.

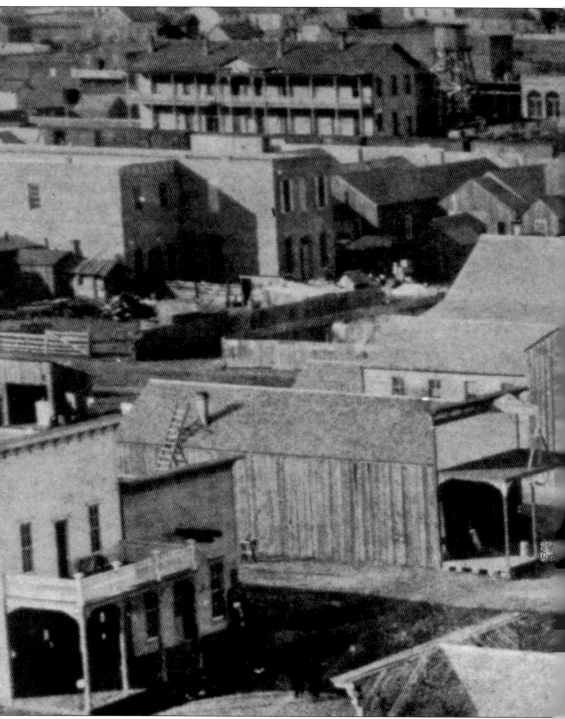
Abilene in 1890 looked like a busy Western town. This picture was taken from the original courthouse in Abilene looking northwest. It shows wagon yards, saloons, hotels, general stores, and the railroad purposefully cutting through the center of town. The town lot sales included

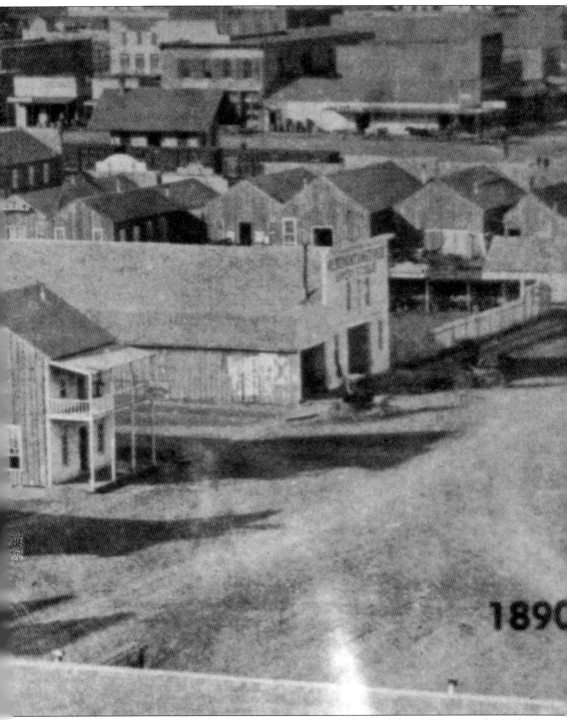

the agreement that one lot had to be sold on the north side of the tracks and the next lot had to be sold on the south side of the tracks. This method insured the growth of the town to be centered around the railroad.

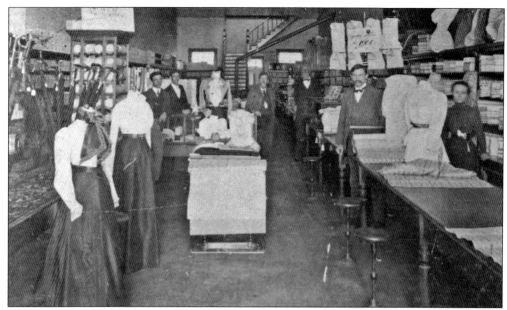

The Minter family was here when Abilene was founded, and Minter's Store was one of the first stores in the town. This picture shows how it looked in 1900. Minter's was Abilene's longest-running department store. It always featured the most up-to-date clothing trends. (Courtesy of the Minter family.)

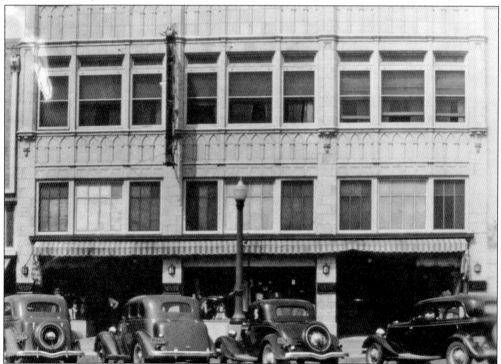

This picture of Minter's was taken in the 1930s on Pine Street. Minter's was one of the first stores to "departmenize" in Abilene, and it had a choice location in downtown Abilene for many years. They finally sold the family business in the late 20th century. (Courtesy of the Minter family.)

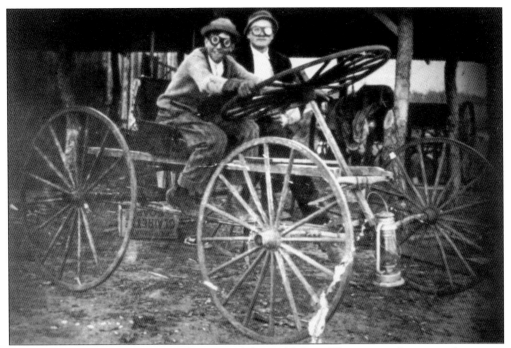

This picture shows the impact of the automobile on Abilene. These young boys must have seen their first automobile and run home to put their "car" together. Complete with goggles and a steering wheel, the boys had a full day of fun in their automobile.

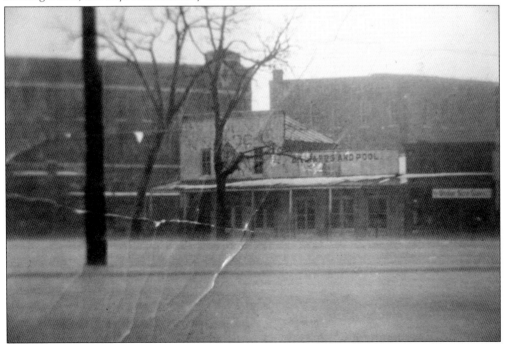

A flood in 1911 nearly wiped out downtown Abilene businesses. This picture shows North First Street between Pine and Cypress Streets. Abilene was mostly flat, and nearly all the downtown businesses received some form of water damage.

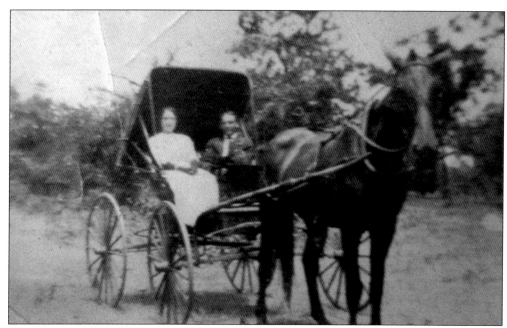

This picture is a good representation of how a man courted in the early days. The businessman and his date would go for a drive in the country in his horse and buggy. Men almost always wore ties, no matter the occasion.

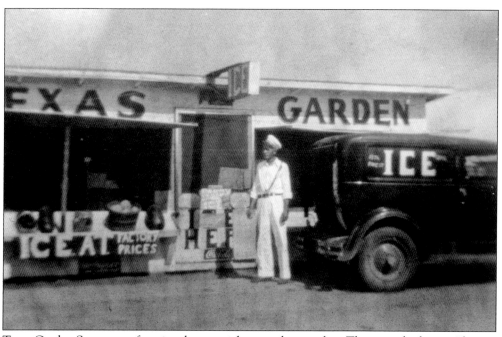

Texas Garden Store was a favorite place to pick up garden supplies. They even had ice at "factory prices." Parking was never a problem; one just drove up to the front door and made purchases. The employees would come right out to help.

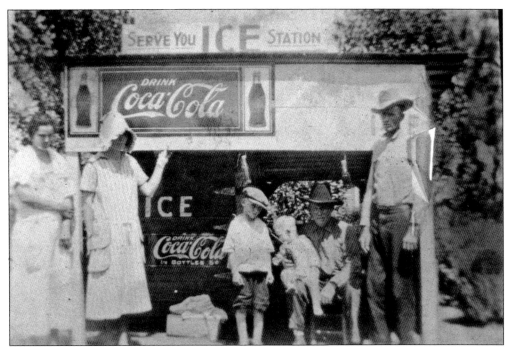

This picture depicts a family refreshment stand. Customers could come up, purchase a soda, and drink it right on the side of the road. Families had to supplement their income any way they could.

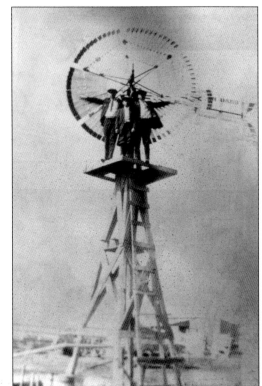

The windmill business was thriving in early Abilene. Here the salesman and a customer enjoy the sights from atop some merchandise. Almost every farm had a windmill to pull water to the surface.

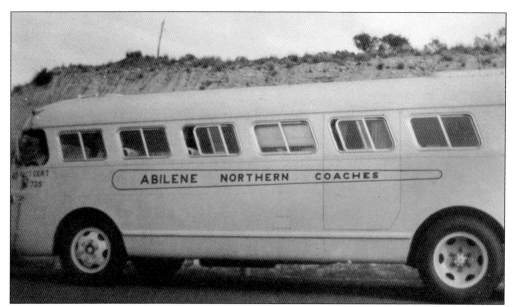

Abilene Northern Coaches was Abilene's very own bus line that operated for several years. Customers were now able to ride in comfort from or to Abilene from surrounding towns. The business maintained stops in several area towns.

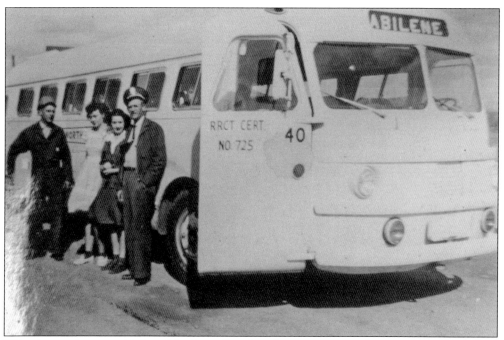

This picture shows an Abilene Northern Coach making a stop to pick up customers. The line also operated routes within Abilene. Note that even back then the drivers were in uniforms with hats.

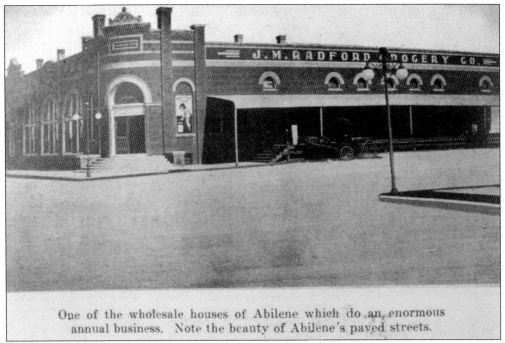

One of the wholesale houses of Abilene which do an enormous annual business. Note the beauty of Abilene's paved streets.

The J. M. Radford Wholesale Grocery was a prosperous business in Abilene for several years. It was located at South First and Oak Streets and served customers in most of West Texas.

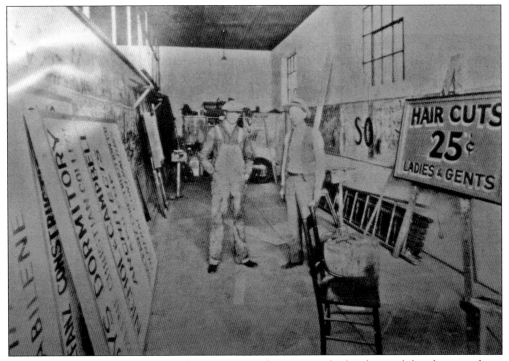

Taggert Sign Company was kept busy trying to keep up with the demand for their products in Abilene. Sign painting was really an art in early Abilene, and talented artists were always in demand.

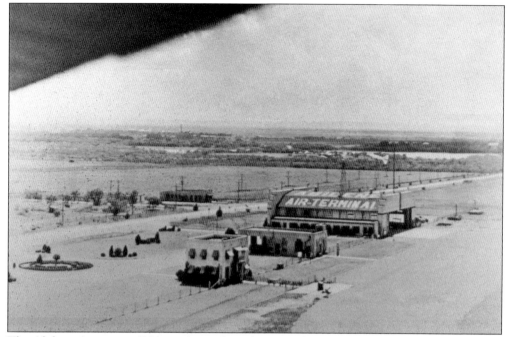

The Abilene Airport in 1934 was located on the east side of town. Flying into and out of this airport in the 1930s was always exciting. Abilene got into the flying business early because of the interest of several of the city's businessmen.

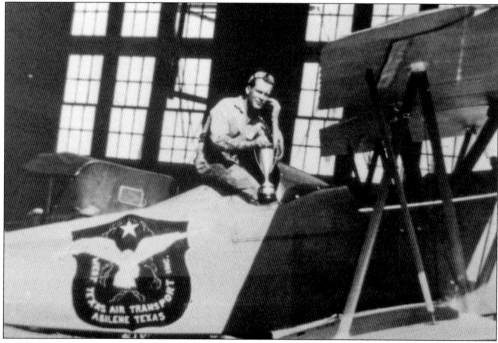

E. L. Derryberry was one of the first aviators in Abilene's history of flying. It was his piqued interest and that of several other businessmen that led the town to even have an airport. He encouraged other businessmen to become pilots.

Abilene received a new airport terminal building in 1948. Flying was here to stay, and Abilene wanted to update its airport. The new control tower helped to make flying in the Abilene area much safer and more reliable.

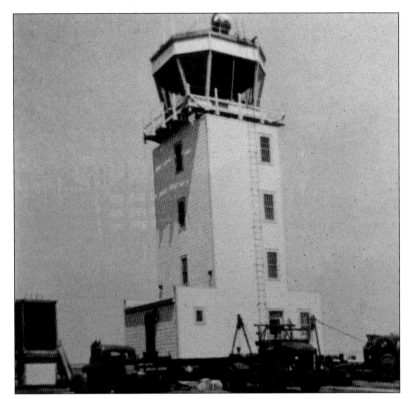

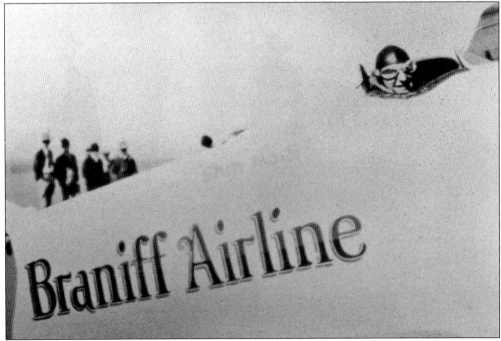

Tom Braniff lifted his airline off the ground and made several stops in Abilene in the 1930s. He could carry three passengers in the plane above. Many people would go to the airport out of curiosity just to see the amazing flying machines.

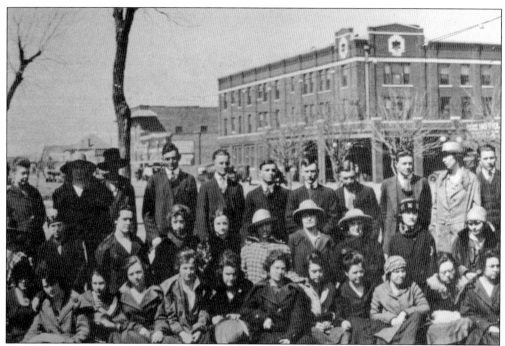

Graduates of one of Abilene's business colleges pose at Everman Park near North First and Pine Streets. The Grace Hotel is in the background of the picture. Abilene business colleges drew students from many surrounding towns for their enrollments. Some of the graduates went on to become business leaders in Abilene and other nearby towns. Note the style of clothing in these pictures.

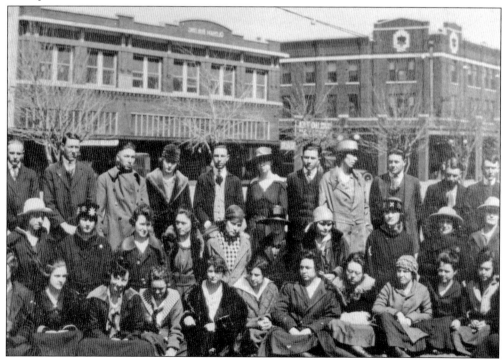

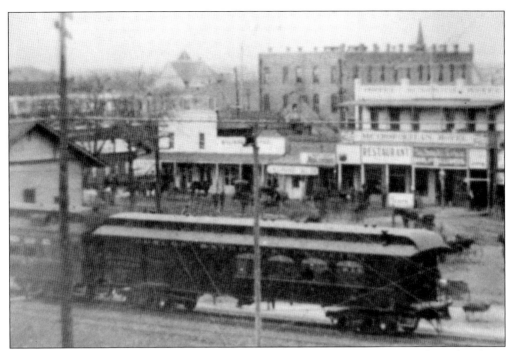

This picture taken around 1890 shows an early passenger car on the train track. It also shows several restaurants and gift stores on North First Street. Trains stopped in Abilene to let the passengers stretch their legs, get something to eat, and visit the stores.

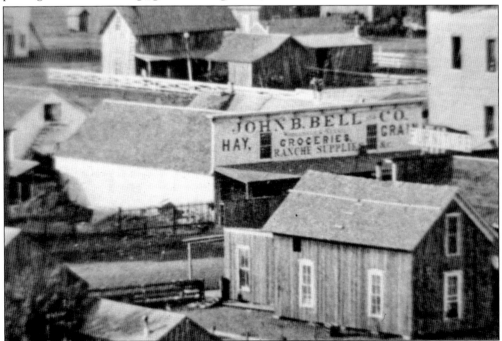

John Bell's store was located at South Second and Sycamore Streets. The store had groceries, saddles, and hardware supplies. Customers could buy grain, hay, and other ranch products there. It was the Walmart of early Abilene.

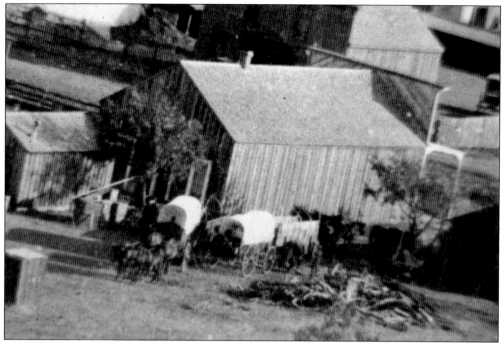

Abilene had several wagon yards in the downtown area. This one shows covered wagons driven by new families arriving in town. It was a custom to drive wagons into wagon yards instead of leaving them on streets. It also shows outhouses that were in use in the early days.

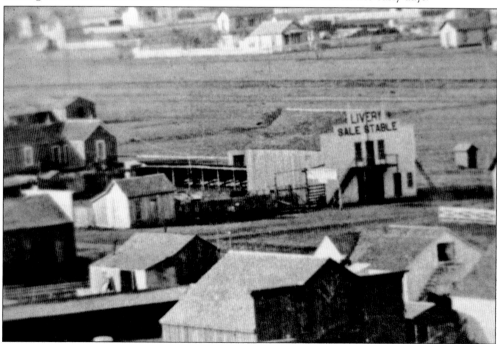

Livery stables were a necessity in early Western towns. Customers could stable, buy, and sell their horses at the local livery stable. This livery was located on the south side of the railroad tracks in downtown Abilene.

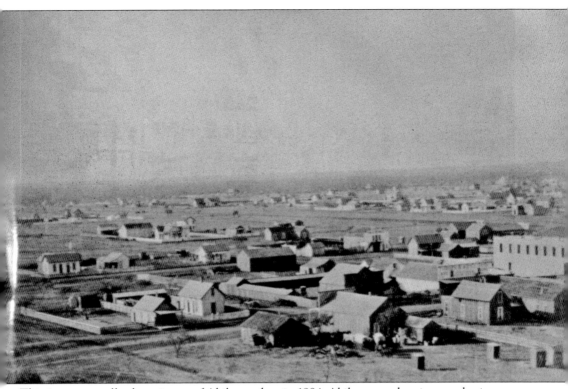

This is an unusually clear picture of Abilene taken in 1884. Abilene was drawing new businesses to the "Future Great City" of West Texas. New families came by covered wagon, horseback, and train, and businesses were opening almost daily to accommodate the growing population. Ranching and farming played a big part in the new city. The trains were full of people moving west in the 1880s. Churches and schools soon followed the growth of the city, which had its share of saloons and bawdy houses, too. The citizens demanded law enforcement and fire protection.

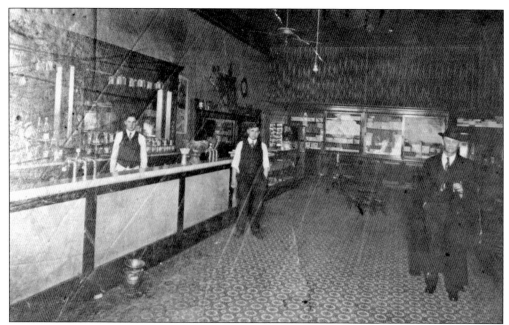

The Ingle Drugstore was located at South First and Chestnut Streets. It was right downtown and a popular drugstore for customers to meet their needs and visit with neighbors. Note the long counter for dispensing drinks and the early dispensing handles. (Courtesy of the Ingle family.)

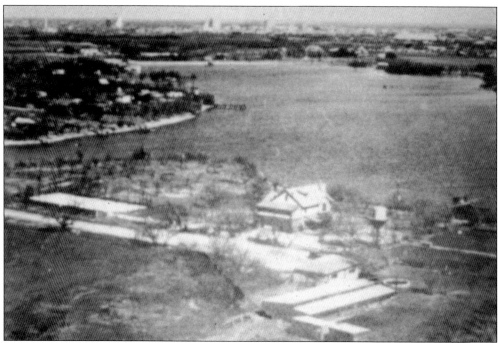

This is one of the first dairy farms in Abilene. It was located southeast of town next to the first lake in Abilene. The two-story brick home is still there today. Abilene was one of the few towns to have its own dairy products produced locally.

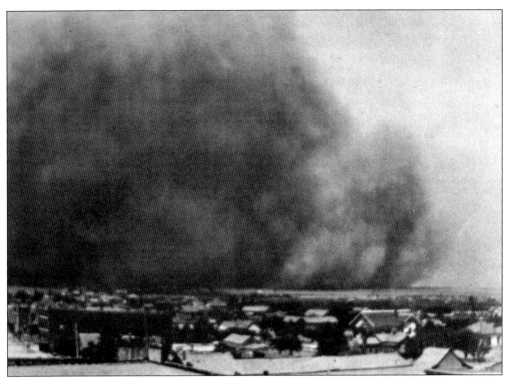

This picture of a 1917 dust storm is a good example of the terrible storms that the pioneers had to weather in the early days of Western towns. These meteorological phenomenons would shut down a town until it blew over. People would head for cover when they knew one was coming.

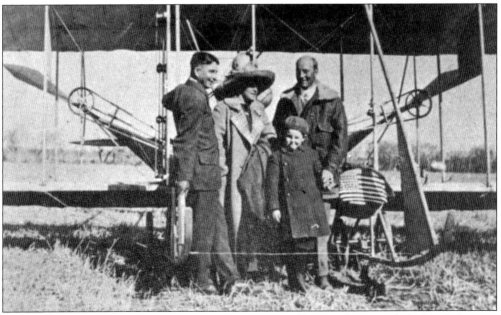

This is the first airplane that landed in Abilene, and it really caused a stir with the locals. It is not known exactly when it landed, but it was a successful operation. It marked the beginning of flying in Abilene. The first pilots had to have a lot of faith in these flying machines to operate them.

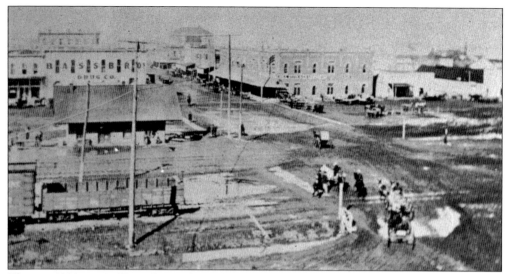

This pre-1900 view of Pine Street shows the railroad crossing and the electrical lines that were installed in 1891, along with the train depot. The federal post office is the tallest building in the background, which was constructed in 1891.

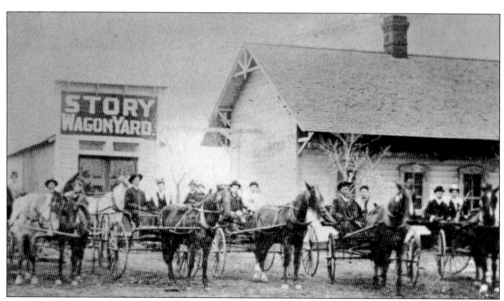

The people here are attending a wedding in Tye, Texas, just on the western edge of Abilene. It must have been a prominent wedding for so many people to show up in their horse-drawn buggies. Note the clothing that people wore to weddings in that day and age.

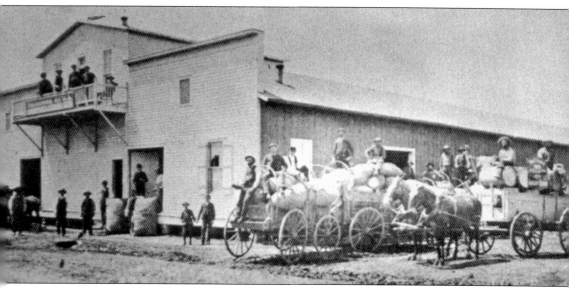
Heyck Shipping Company was located at North First and Cypress Streets. The early freight and shipping companies played a big part in settling early Abilene. They were responsible for loading and unloading freight cars on the railroad. They also employed several people to handle the large volume of business that early Abilene saw. All the supplies that came into Abilene were handled by companies like this. Families employed these companies to unload their belongings from freight cars and get them to their new homes as soon as they were built.

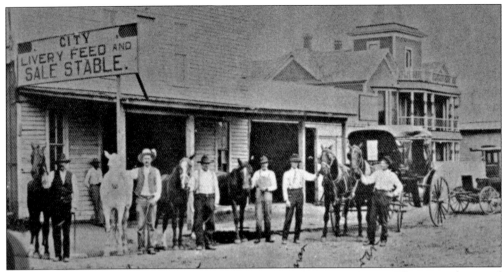

City Livery Feed and Sale Stable was located at 204 North Cypress Street. This is another good example of an early livery business in Abilene. This livery was located right in downtown Abilene in the early 1890s. Note the type of clothes that workers wore while on the job.

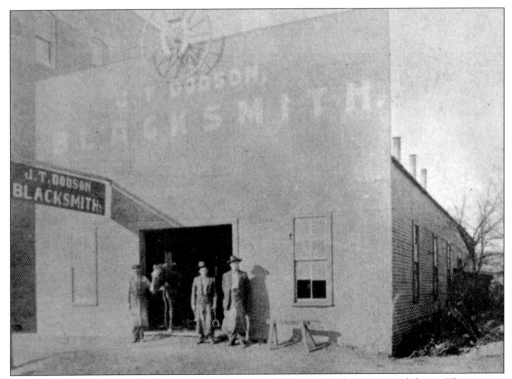

The J. D. Dodson Blacksmith business was an early day establishment in Abilene. Their main business was shoeing horses and repairing wagons. When the automobile came along, it put a lot of blacksmiths out of business. Early Western towns could not do without a good blacksmith.

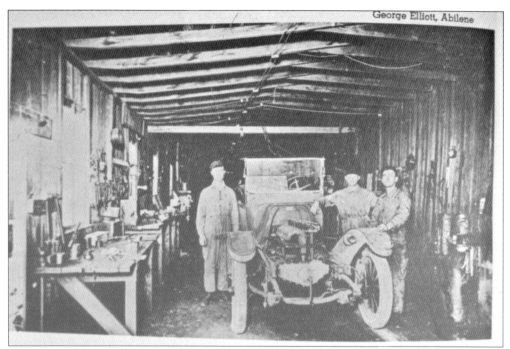

The C. B. Manly Garage was located at 1143 South Third Street. When people saw that the automobile was here to stay, garages opened to service these new modes of transportation. People had to be trained to service automobiles, and new businesses opened to cater to this need.

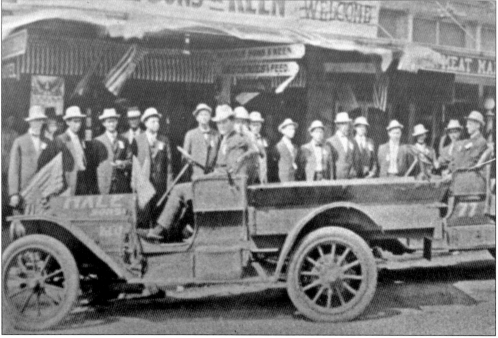

Hale Grocery was located at 146 Cypress Street. This picture was taken in front of the grocery showing off a new delivery truck, which was a new service that grocery stores provided to their customers. Hale Grocery was prominent in Abilene for many years.

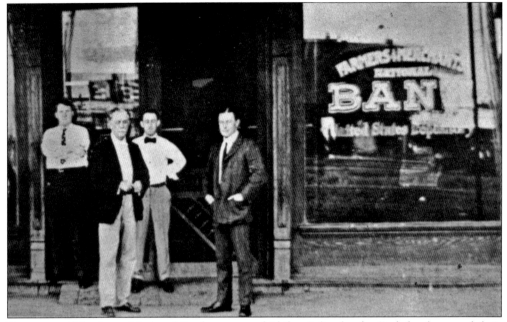

Farmers and Merchants National Bank was one of Abilene's first banks. Early banks served their customers as they do today, but with a lot less red tape. This bank continues today in Abilene and is rated one of the best in the whole nation.

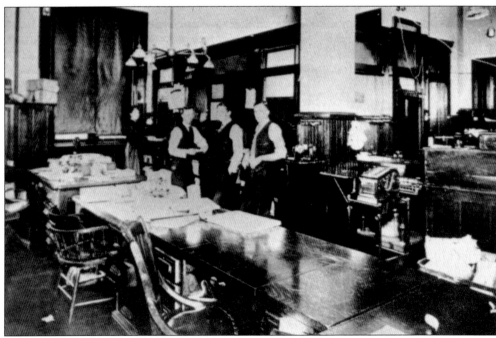

This is a picture behind the scenes at the federal post office in Abilene in 1915. Even a growing town like Abilene had a large volume of mail and packages coming through the post office. Note how the furniture was arranged to handle the everyday business.

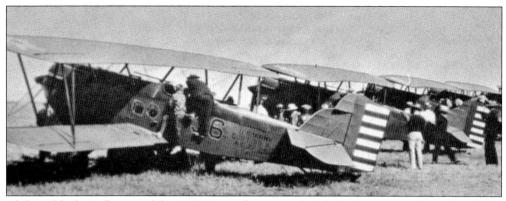

Abilene felt the influence of the U.S. Army when several of their planes came through in 1928. Abilene, due to its good weather and location, has always had the interests of the military. Later Camp Barkeley, an army base, was located in Abilene during World War II. Dyess Air Force Base, founded in 1957, is still located in Abilene today.

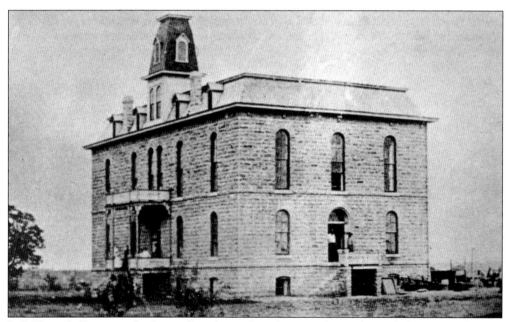

Bell Plain College was the first college located in this area. It was located about 25 miles east of Abilene. It was in operation from 1881 until 1888, when outside pressures caused it to close. Abilene soon closed the gap with the West Texas Baptist College.

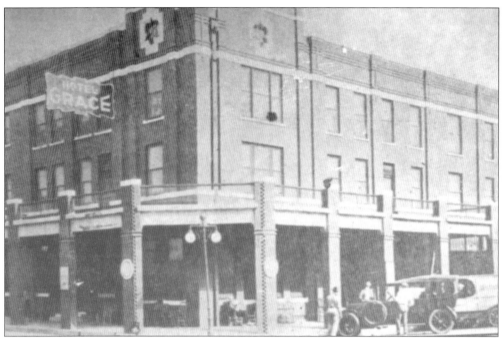

The Grace Hotel was located in the 100 block of Cypress Street. This picture was taken before 1926 when a fourth floor was added. It was located across the street from the train depot, so many people spent their first night in Abilene at the Grace Hotel. It is called the Grace Museum today.

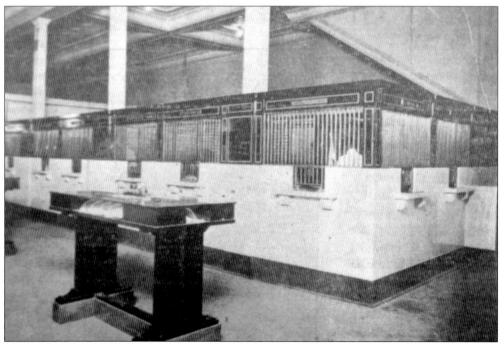

The First State Bank was another bank that served early Abilene. This picture shows the lobby area; tellers were separated from their customers by metal bars in those years. Banks were responsible for keeping the financial part of the Abilene economy in a healthy position.

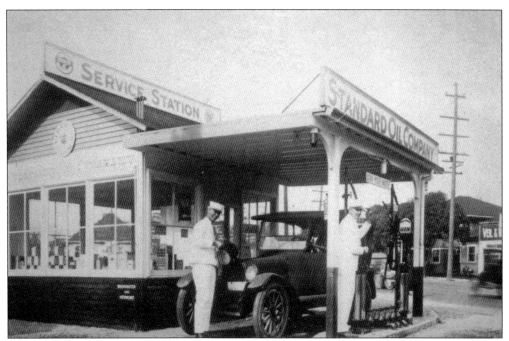

This picture of an early service station is a classic. Service stations were just beginning to start operating with the arrival of the automobile. Note the uniforms of the men and the hats they wore. A customer really received personal service from these early stations.

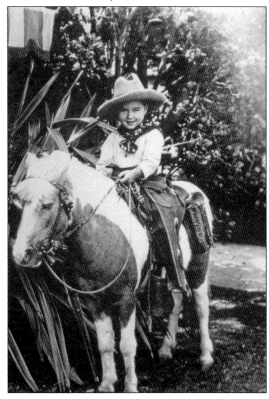

Even the kids in early Abilene got to dress up as cowboys and ride ponies around the neighborhood. Children made up more of their own fun and games before all the electronics of today.

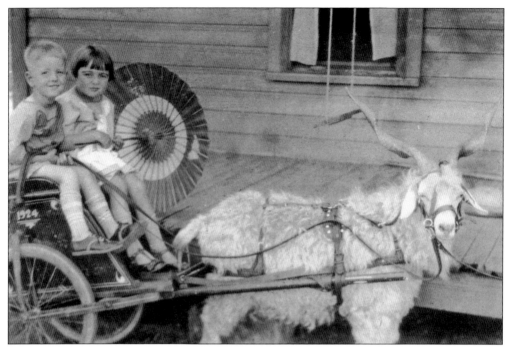

This is another good example of what kids were able to do when they put their minds to having fun. Parents could go to hardware stores to buy the supplies needed to put these buggies together, inspiring family fun without the benefit of television, theaters, or electronic games.

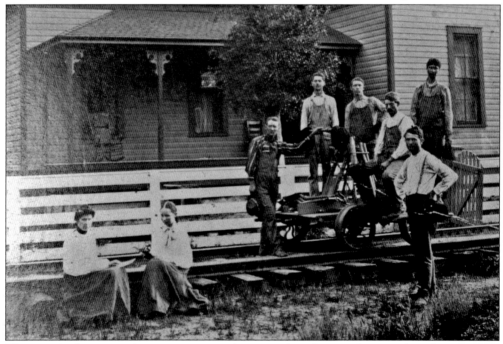

This picture shows a work crew on a manual pump railcar. It is not known whose house was so close to the tracks, but the family was surely kept awake when a train traveled past. Note the style of clothing that the workmen wore for that type of work.

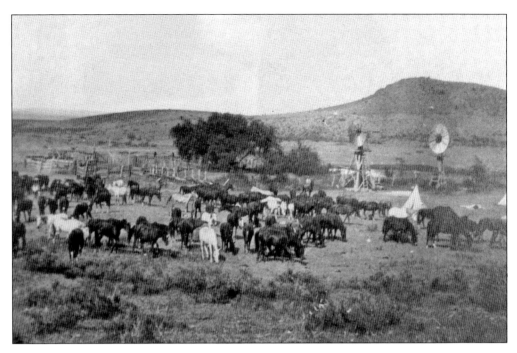

Transportation in the West depended on the horse. It did not matter whether one lived in the city or on a ranch, horses were very important. A horse camp is shown here on a ranch near Abilene, where ranchers had to keep extra horses for their cowboys. People took care of their horses, because they depended on them for their transportation. When a horse sale took place, there were always people there to buy and sell their horses.

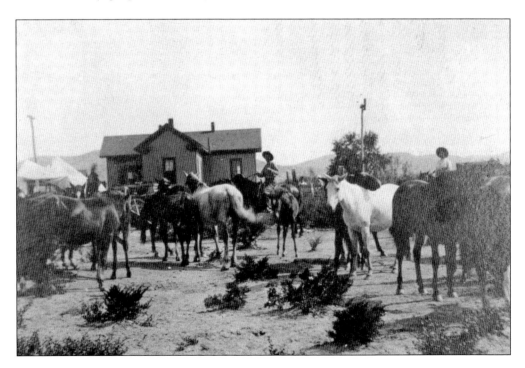

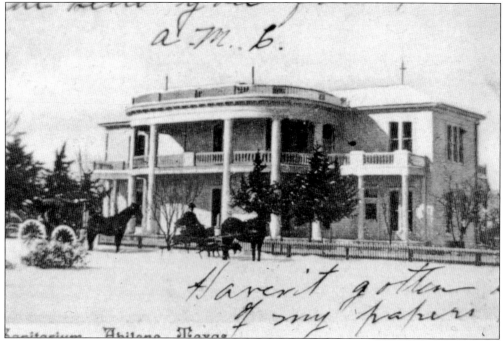

Alexander Sanitarium was one of the first hospitals between Fort Worth and El Paso. Dr. Jim Alexander was the hospital's founder and head doctor. The hospital also served as a training school for nurses, located on North Sixth Street, just west of the downtown area.

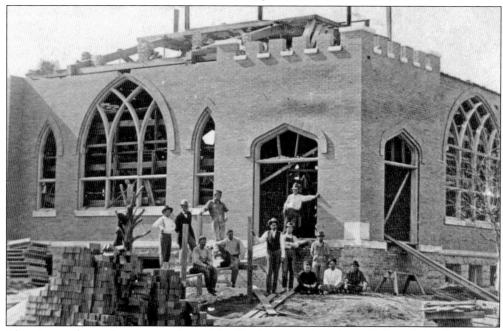

The picture shows the construction of the Presbyterian church in Abilene. The church was located at the corner of North Second and Beech Streets. The Presbyterians were the first congregation to form a church in Abilene. Early congregations met in homes or businesses until a church could be built.

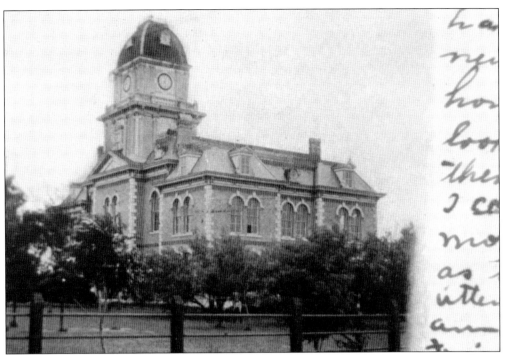

Soon after the election to move the county seat from Buffalo Gap to Abilene, a new courthouse was built on the south side of Oak Street. This structure served the county well for several years before it was torn down and a new courthouse was built.

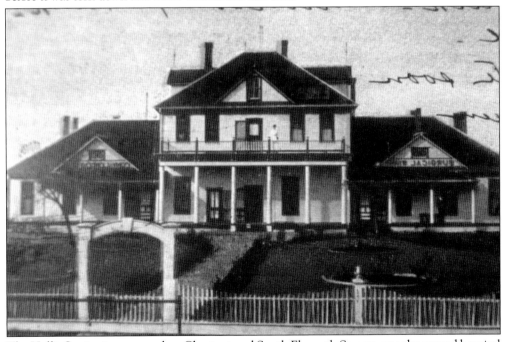

The Hollis Sanitarium, erected on Chestnut and South Eleventh Streets, was the second hospital built in Abilene. There were not too many early towns that could claim to have two hospitals. These hospitals were able to care for the people of Abilene for several years.

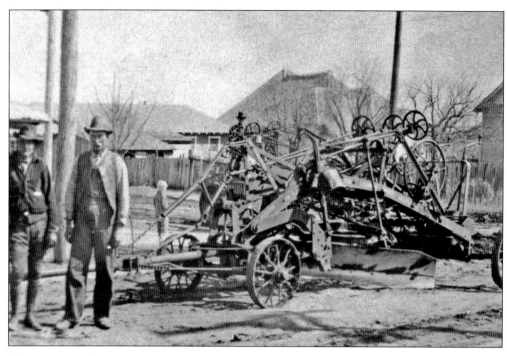

These pictures show some the equipment the city used in maintaining the streets of Abilene in 1924. Tractors pulled the street grader. Since most of the downtown streets were paved in 1911, the equipment was upgraded to handle paved streets. Most of the other streets were still dirt. City crews had to work on the dirt streets constantly to keep them in usable condition. Modern equipment was slow to arrive in the small town.

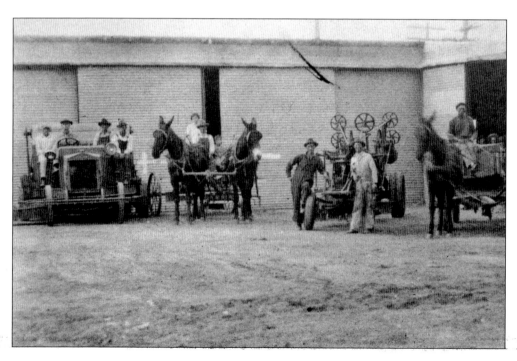

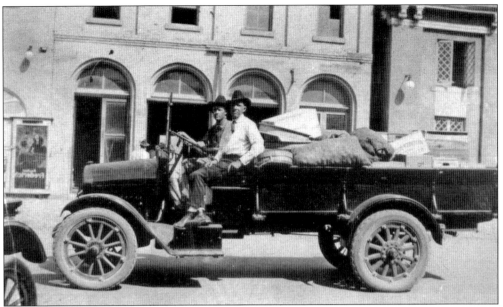

Grocery delivery trucks such as this one took over for the horse-drawn buggies that delivered to customers for several years. The advent of the automobile in West Texas changed many things for businesses.

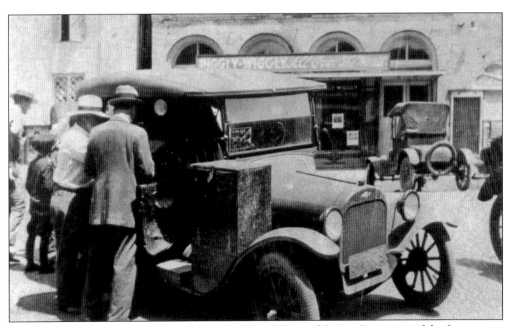

The Piggy Wiggly grocery store was located on North Second Street. It was one of the few grocery stores that was right downtown. Note the old cars and some of the "extras" that were put on the sides of the cars back then.

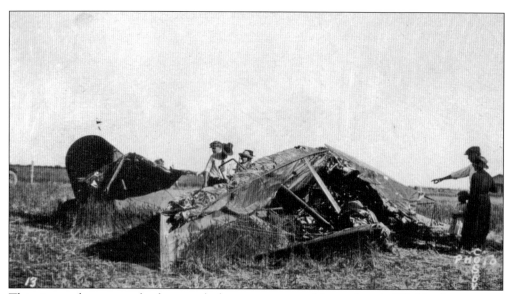

This picture shows an early plane crash that was not moved from where it fell. The first airports did not have the best landing strips. They were dirt and not kept in the best shape. Several planes crashed because of the conditions of the strips.

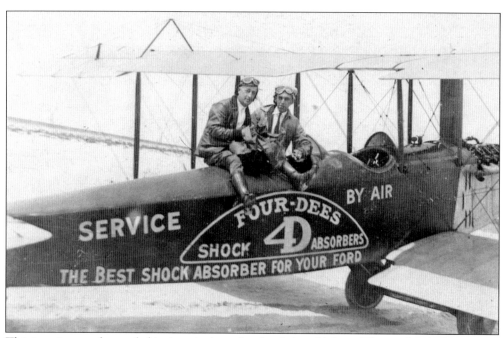

This is a picture of an early bi-wing airplane that landed in Abilene. These pilots had a sponsor that helped with the expenses of flying the plane around the country. These planes were an immediate attraction wherever they landed.

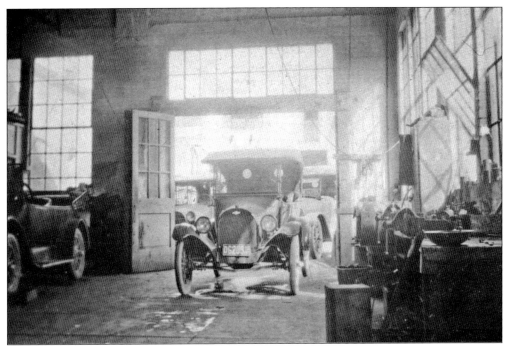

The Chevrolet dealership was located on North Second Street. The first dealerships were not as attractive on the inside as they are today. The customer areas were not clean, but they got the job done.

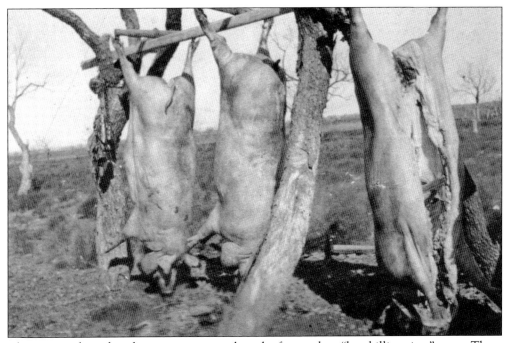

This picture shows how hogs were processed on the farms when "hog killing time" came. There was no refrigeration available, so hogs were delivered to the butcher, where they processed the animals, and finally sent to the customer.

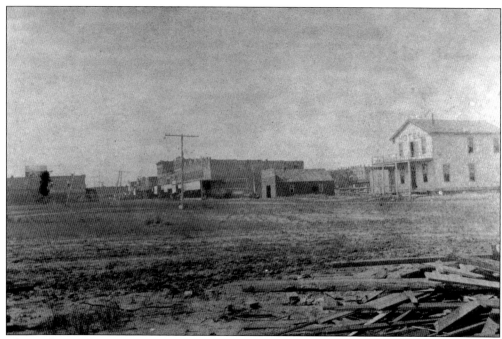

This is the northern boundary of the business district in 1893. This is North Fourth and Pine Streets. These are the first buildings and businesses that were located on Pine Street. They were all wood construction and burned down almost on a regular basis.

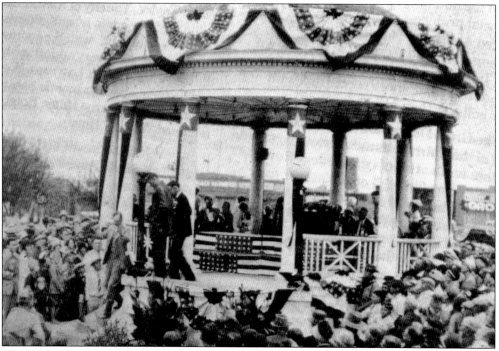

Charles Lindbergh flew into Abilene in 1928 after his famous trip across the Atlantic Ocean. He gave a speech at the bandstand behind the post office in downtown Abilene before flying on to his next stop.

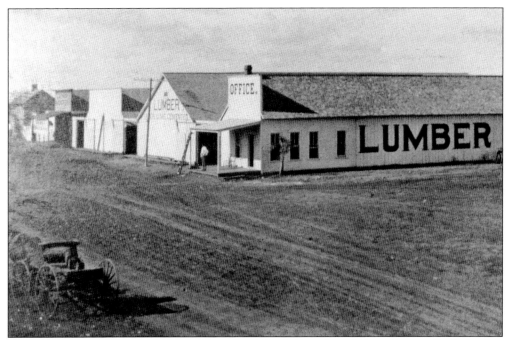

West Texas Lumber Company was located at North Fourth and Pine Streets. Early lumber companies like this one were kept busy. The trains would bring the lumber to town, and it was freighted to the companies that had customers ready to purchase the lumber and supplies.

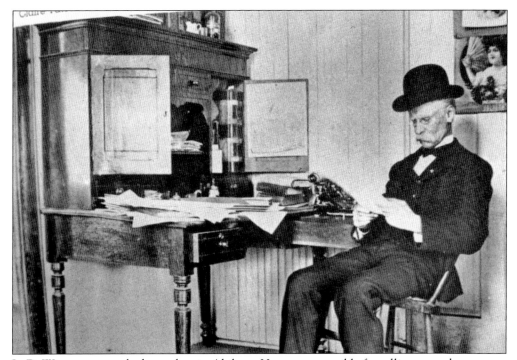

L. D. Wise was an early day realtor in Abilene. He was responsible for selling several new areas in the town. He controlled over 500 lots in Abilene at one time.

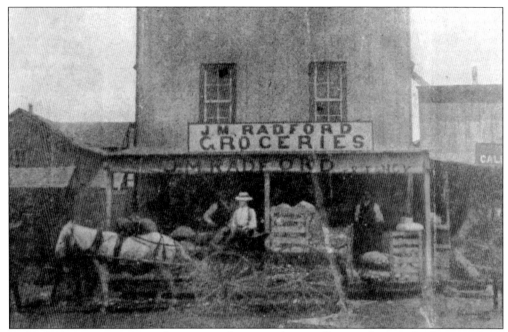

Radford Grocery, as seen in this picture, began with a small store that was built into a large wholesale operation. This is the first store that J. M. Radford had in early Abilene. He was a man who knew how to expand, and he ended up with one of the largest wholesale grocery businesses in West Texas.

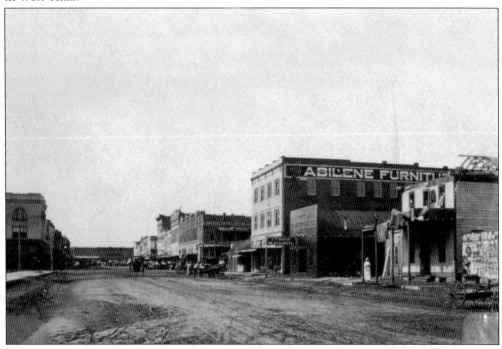

This picture shows Pine Street in 1891. Note the building on the right, which had been in a fire. Many wooden buildings burned in Abilene before volunteer firemen could reach the scene. Electricity was introduced in 1891, but the streets were not paved until 1911.

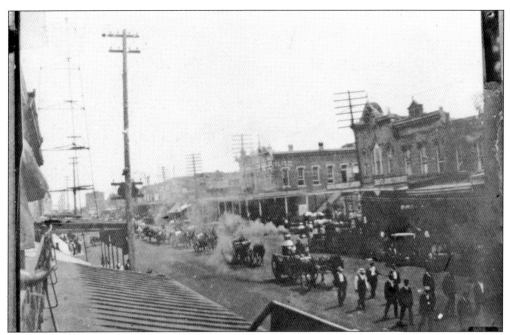

In this rather clear picture, a parade is marching down the streets of Abilene. Note the tall poles that carried electricity to the downtown area. The electric company had many problems when it first tried electricity. The system was not dependable, so people kept their oil-burning lamps for quite a while.

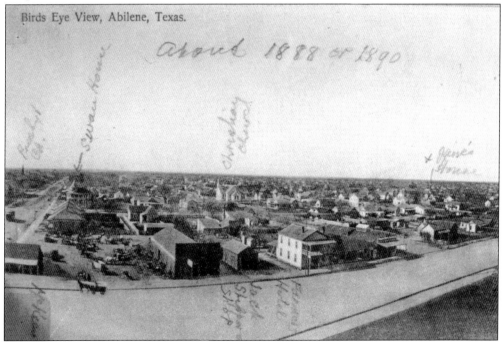

This picture was taken from the courthouse on the south side of downtown looking north. The photographer tried to label some of the structures. Photographs like this allow people to see what Abilene looked like in 1888.

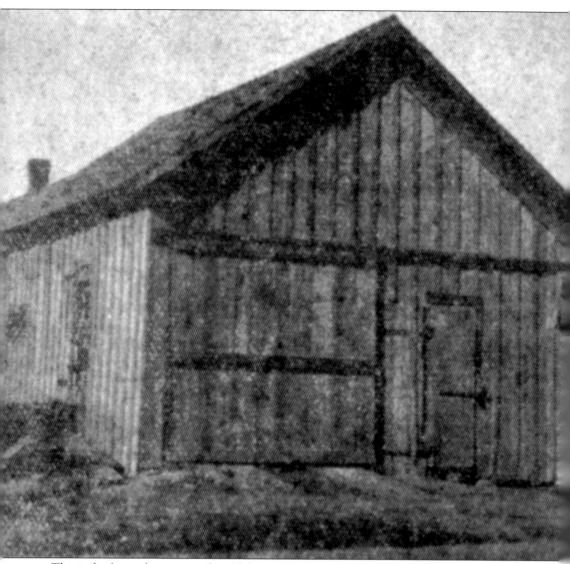

This is the first jail constructed in Abilene in 1885. Abilene was a typical Wild West town in its early days. This building would not win any awards for outstanding jail, but it served its purpose in 1885. The picture below is the jail that replaced this one. This jail was built better and maintained by the city. It held many more prisoners and had a larger staff to operate the jail.

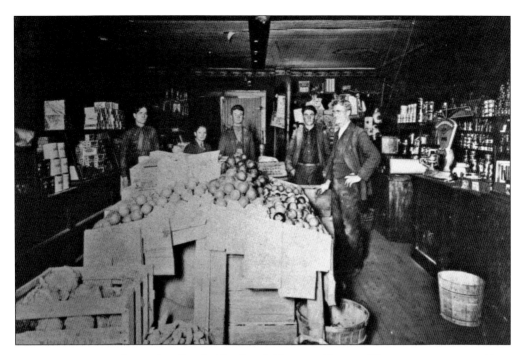

Rogers Grocery was located at South Third and Chestnut Streets. This picture is an excellent example of the inside of an early grocery store. Their products were simply displayed, and the family was there to help their customers. The family opened up another store at North Seventh and Pine Streets. The buildings were simple in construction and were not insulated, except for newspapers stuffed between the walls. Most stores offered home delivery with their personal wagons.

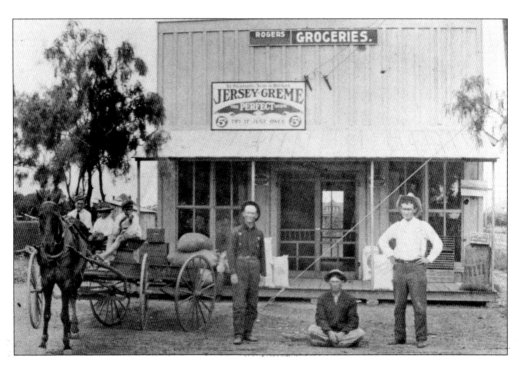

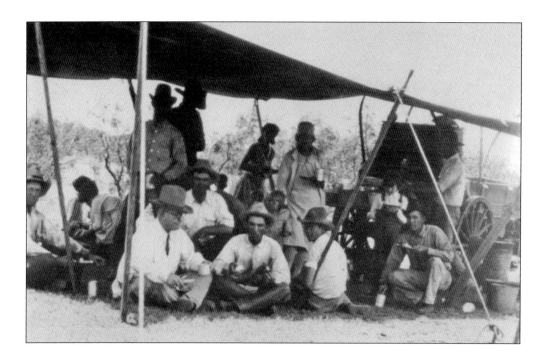

When it was lunchtime out on the range, cowboys looked forward to not only eating, but to also getting out of the sun. Life as a cowboy was not easy in the 1880s and earlier. The chuck wagon enabled the cowboy to eat where he worked. The picture below is undated, but it depicts branding time on the ranch. Cowboys did not have the equipment they do today. It was all hard, dirty work.

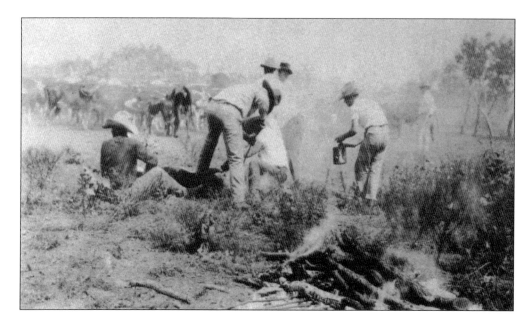

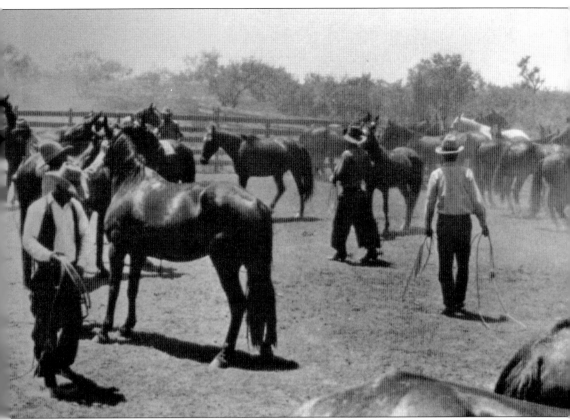

This is a good example of cowboys going out to the corral and picking the horse they wanted to ride that day. Every cowboy had several favorite horses he liked for the different kinds of work being done that day. A good cow horse could work the cattle and save the cowboy a lot of energy. Some were good roping horses, and others could drive the cattle better. The cowboys learned to trust the horse's instincts.

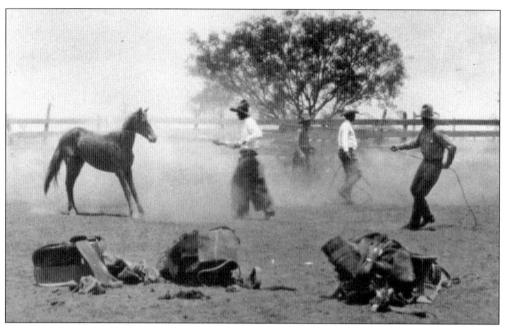

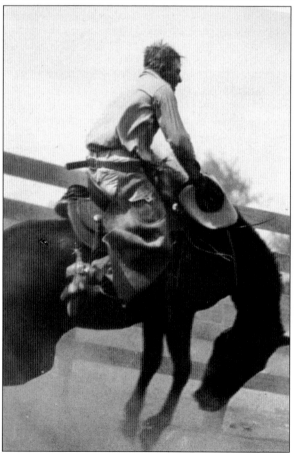

Cowboys had to "break" or tame young horses to work on the ranch. Some cowboys were better bronc busters than others. A good bronc buster would travel to various ranches to help break the horses. Every cowboy had his own system for breaking horses. Some were gentle, but most did it the hard way. They would rope, secure, and get on the best way they could.

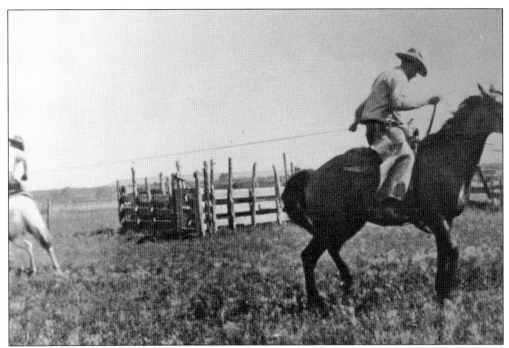

The cowboy's rope was his most important piece of equipment. Every cowboy had his own way of preparing his rope. In this picture, two cowboys are stretching a rope in order to get it to the quality that the cowboy wanted. He would not use it until he thought it was ready.

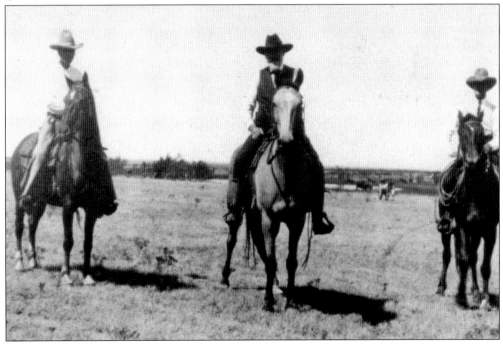

Andrew John Swenson was the manager of the Swenson ranch. He would ride out to check on the cattle and the cowboys. When the boss came out, the cowboys made sure they were doing what they were supposed to be doing and doing it the right way.

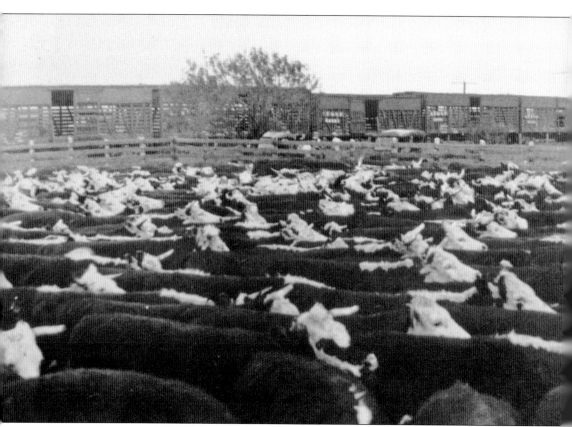

When the train reached West Texas, it put an end to the famous cattle drives. Herefords replaced the days of the Longhorn cattle. When the cattlemen saw how much more meat the Hereford cattle had compared to the Longhorn, they replaced the Longhorn as soon as they could with the Herefords. Shipping your cattle out to market was the ending procedure of the business of ranching.

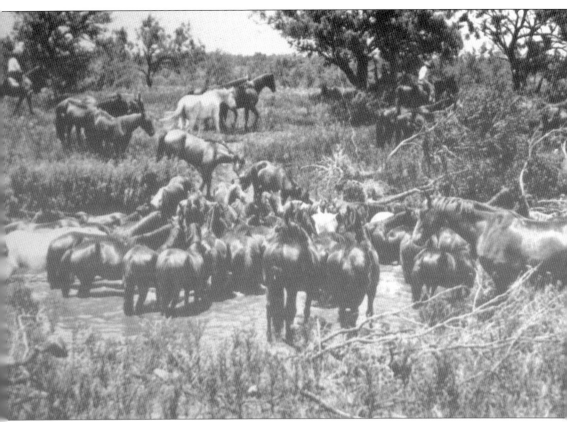

Give a cowboy a good horse and a rope and he could do his job, regardless of the weather. Keeping horses available was just as important as any part of the job for a cowboy. Here a cowboy has driven a herd of horses to a watering hole. Usually the ramada, extra horses for the cowboys, was driven right along with the herd of cattle. Certain cowboys were responsible for keeping the ramada moving and watching over them at night.

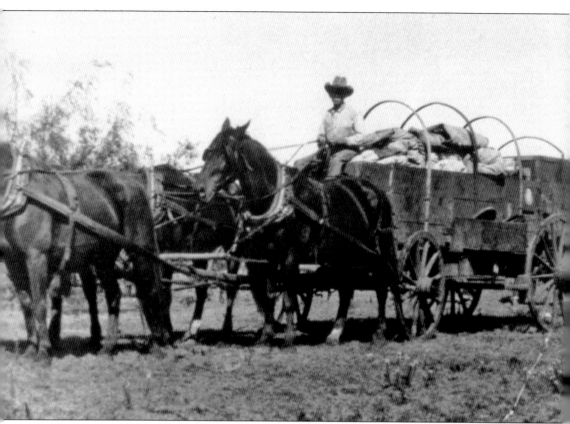

The chuck wagon made trail drives possible. The first trail drives tried to use mules to carry their supplies, but this did not work because there were too many problems. When the chuck wagon was created, these problems were solved, and the trail drives really got started. The cook then had all the implements and supplies he needed right at hand, and the wagon could ford or cross rivers, could be set up anywhere, and provided a reliable source for feeding the cowboys.

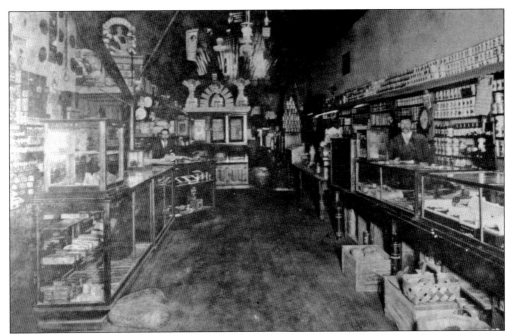

This 1900 picture of the Wiltshire Grocery Store is a good example of an early grocery store. Note the methods of displaying goods; everything was in reach of the customer, and there were several employees to help collect purchases for them.

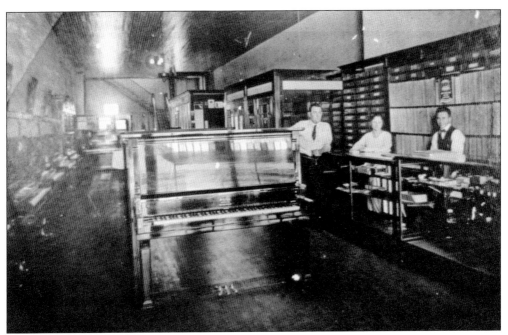

The McDaniel Music Company was one of the first music stores in Abilene. Now customers could buy musical instruments in a store instead of ordering them in a catalogue. Students could decide what instrument they wanted without making a wrong choice and being stuck with it. (Courtesy of the McDaniel family.)

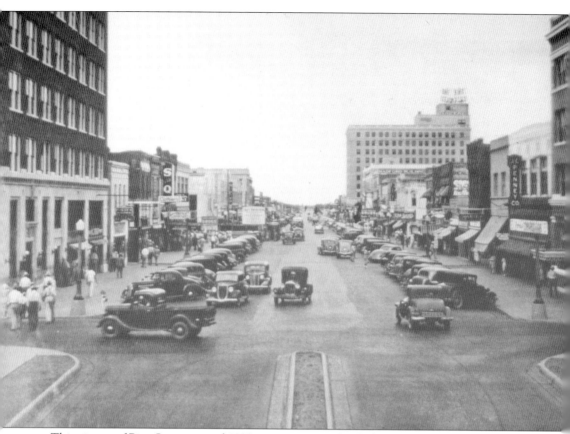

This picture of Pine Street around 1930 is a great example of what a main street looked like. The automobile had taken over the horse by then, and parking downtown was made much easier. Pine Street had become the main location of businesses. The citizens felt safe downtown and could shop at their leisure. Theaters were popular, and parents could let their children go to shows and not worry about them. Restaurants were also popular meeting places for neighbors and friends.

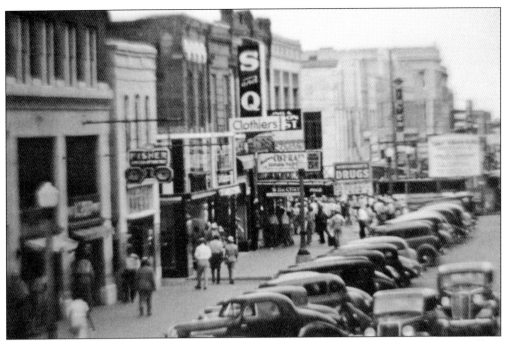
This is the west side of the 100 block of Pine Street around 1930. It was like a shopping mall on the street. Note some of the signs of different businesses that were downtown. Business was good, and the citizens felt safe doing their shopping.

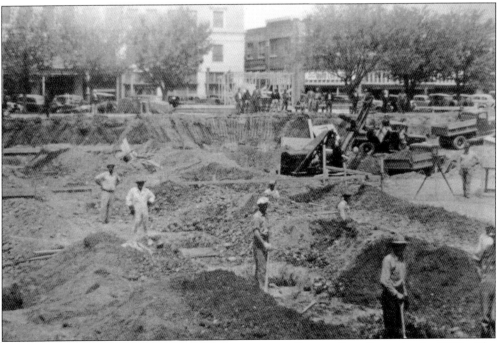
This picture shows the construction of the new post office on Pine Street in the 1930s. The original post office was built in 1891, and the town was ready for a new and larger one. This post office was enlarged several times and still serves Abilene today.

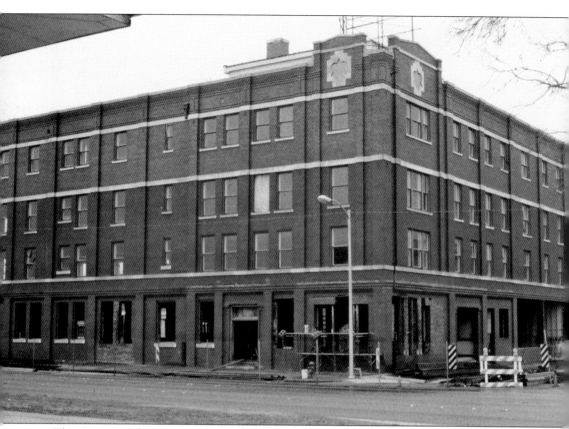

The Grace Hotel was one of the first large hotels in downtown Abilene. It was called the Drake Hotel for a period of time. It originally had three floors, but a fourth floor was added in 1926 with the availability for dancing on the roof. Due to the cost of maintenance, the hotel sat vacant for several years. Today it houses three museums and rental space for various socials and events. It is a showplace downtown that displays what citizens can do to preserve history.

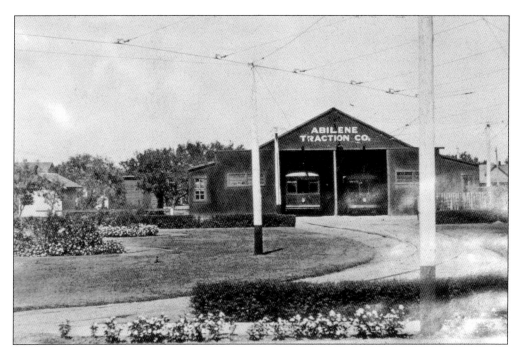

Abilene Traction Company served the town for nearly 30 years. This building was their main service location at North Eleventh and Clinton Streets. The streetcar tracks were not pulled up, but were paved over instead. The town had a streetcar system that covered most of the town. As seen in the photograph below, the streetcars ran on a system of overhead electric wires. People were very accustomed to using the system in Abilene.

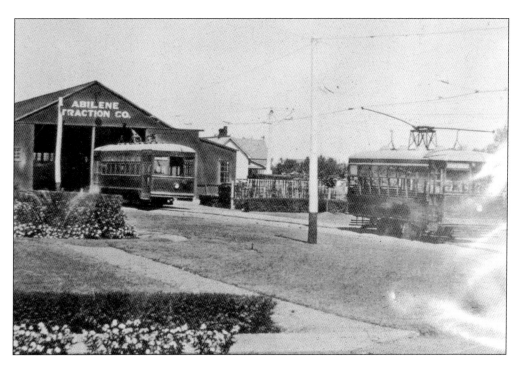

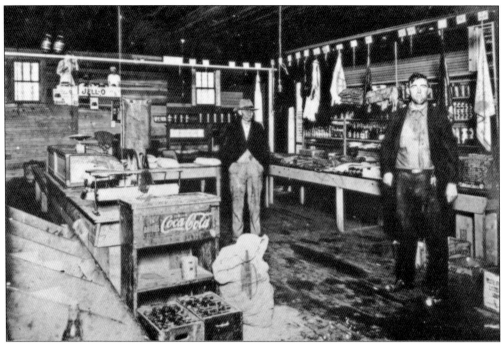

One of the earliest stores in Abilene was Ben Cohen's store. Note that some of the products in the store were displayed in the containers that they were shipped in. There is even an early display case from Coca-Cola. (Courtesy of the Cohen family.)

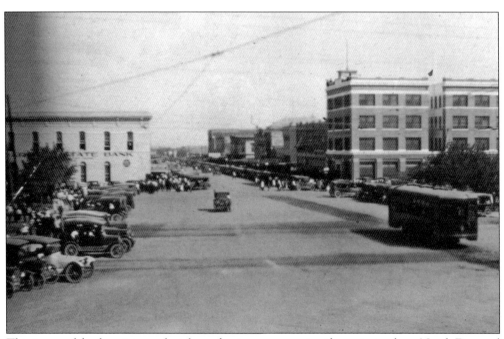

This is one of the few pictures that showed a streetcar crossing the train tracks at North First and Pine Street in 1918. The two buildings facing each other on Pine Street were banks that kept the center of business downtown in 1918.

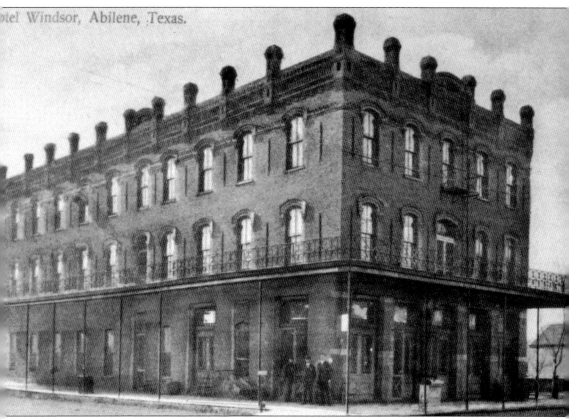

This picture of the original Windsor Hotel at North Second and Cypress Streets shows in detail the character of the hotel. Each chimney on the roof of the building actually went to an individual room in the hotel. It was one of the earliest hotels in the town. People met at hotels in Abilene every morning for coffee and reading the newspaper. Today the building has been restored and houses a gift shop on the first floor, the chamber of commerce on the second floor, and the Abilene Industrial Foundation on the third floor.

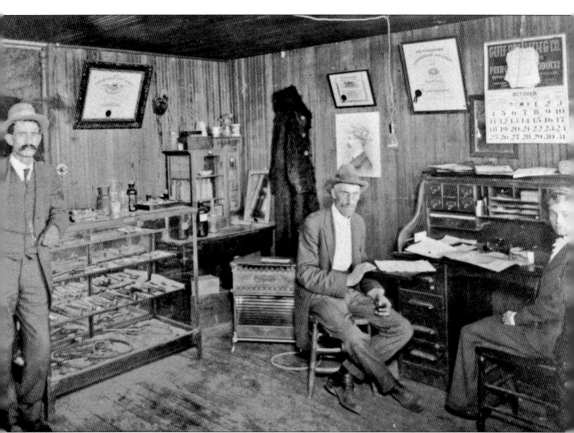

This is a good example of how a businessman's office looked prior to 1900. W. T. Wilson Transfer Company's space was a typical office in early Abilene. Note how things were displayed and the heater was on the floor. All the floors were wooden, and the walls were plain. (Courtesy of the Wilson family.)

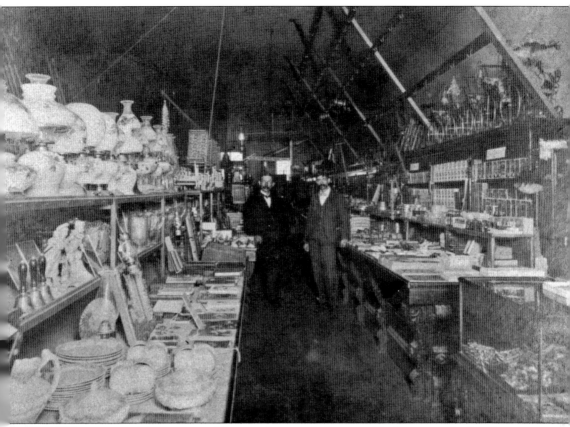

W. T. Wilson operated this store in addition to his transfer business. Products were displayed very simply for the customer. Note that the handbells and oil-burning lamps were still in demand in 1914. (Courtesy of the Wilson family.)

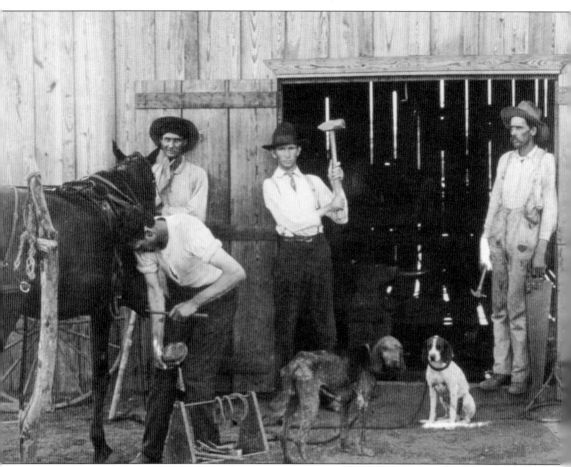

This picture shows an early horseshoeing business in Abilene. Keeping shoes on horses was a full-time business. Horses were the main transportation method before automobiles, and they had to be kept in good health, and shoeing was part of that process. Note the early buildings had no insulation and very little protection from the weather. Shoeing was a backbreaking chore, and only the strongest men took on the task. At this time in history, there were only simple tools and very little conveniences to work with at this kind of business.

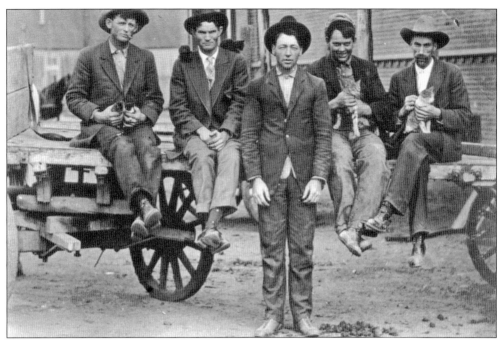

Employees of W. T. Wilson Transfer Company posed for this picture. Note the clothing the men wore, and only one of the men had a tie on in the picture. Businesses kept cats around to keep down the rodent population. (Courtesy of the Wilson family.)

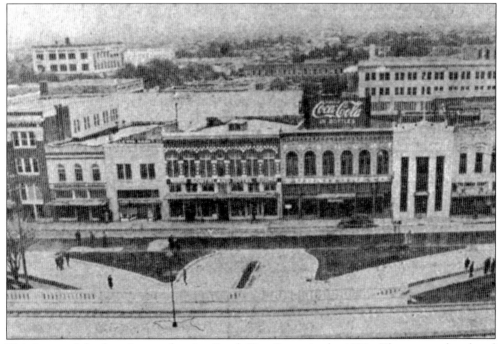

This is one of the few pictures showing South First Street in the 1930s. There was a hotel and a theater among the businesses on this block that faced the train tracks. This whole block was done away with when the underpasses were built.

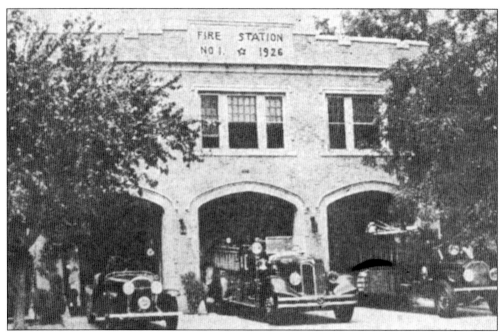

This fire station was constructed in 1926, and it was located at North Fourth and Cedar Streets for several years. This station provided protection for most of the downtown area. It was one of the first stations to provide housing for the firemen on duty.

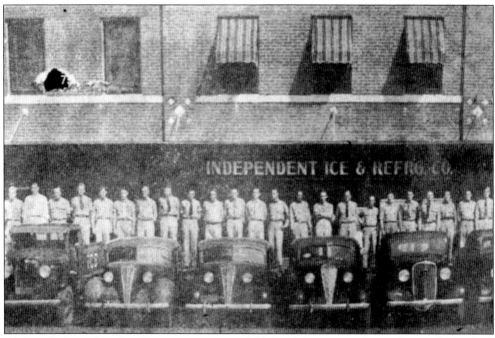

Abilene Independent Ice Company was one of Abilene's largest employers. It was their job to make and distribute ice to businesses and homes. For many years, ice caused sickness because it was not purified, but it became safe when companies like this one opened.

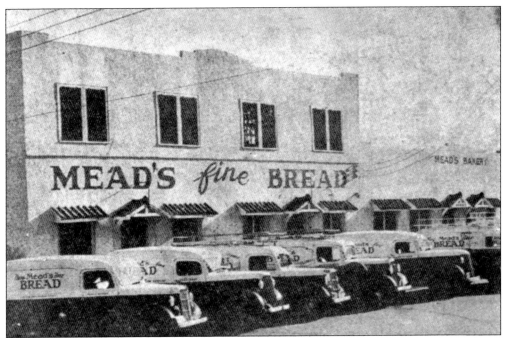

Mead's Fine Bread was another family-owned business. Fresh bread was a staple that was always in demand. This company grew and branched out in West Texas. They had a fleet of delivery trucks at their disposal.

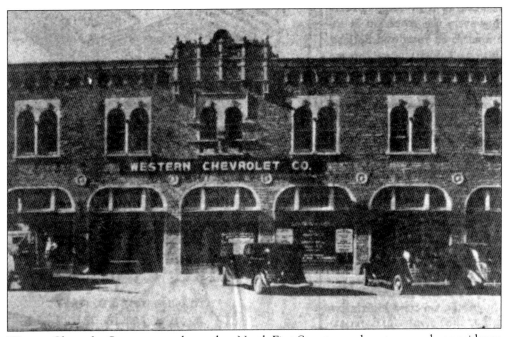

Western Chevrolet Company was located on North First Street near downtown and was evidence that automobile dealerships were moving into better buildings and better showrooms. Today this building houses a furniture warehouse.

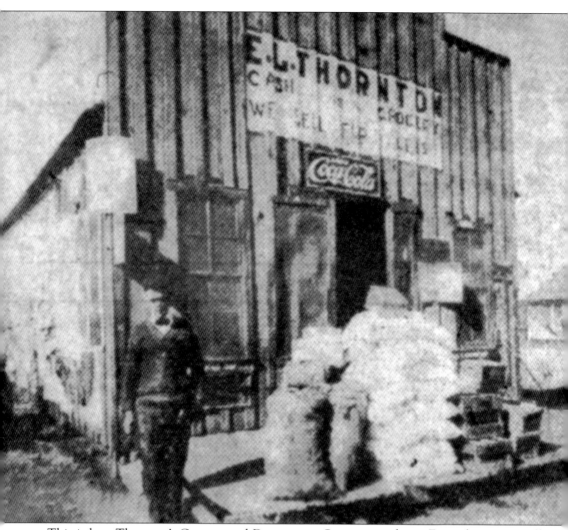

This is how Thornton's Grocery and Department Stores started out. From this very small beginning, Thornton's grew to a large department store and had several locations in Abilene and surrounding towns. If someone had something to barter with, Thornton's would trade. E. L. Thornton was ahead of his time when it came to building a business. He expanded his store to take up an entire city block. It was truly a department store. The store even sold automobiles. He expanded to several locations in Abilene and several area towns.

Three
ENTERTAINMENT IN EARLY ABILENE

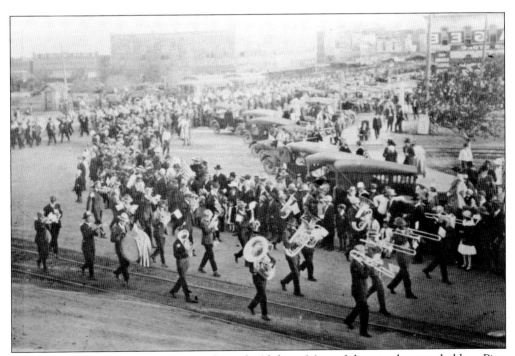

Parades were the main entertainment for early Abilene. Most of the parades were held on Pine and Cypress Streets, and the general public always turned out to watch. Parades were held for several purposes: some were for entertainment and some were for other reasons such as politics.

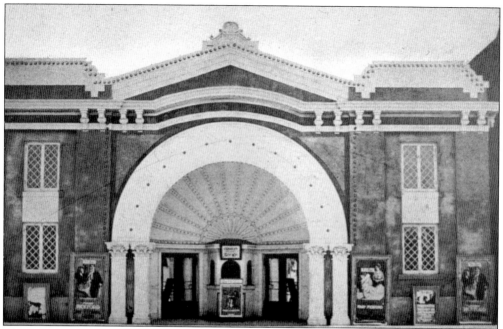

The Queen Theater was located on North Second and Cypress Streets. It was not one of the first, but it stayed open for several decades in downtown Abilene. A ticket cost 10¢, and one could purchase popcorn for 5¢. Early movies were very popular and always drew a crowd.

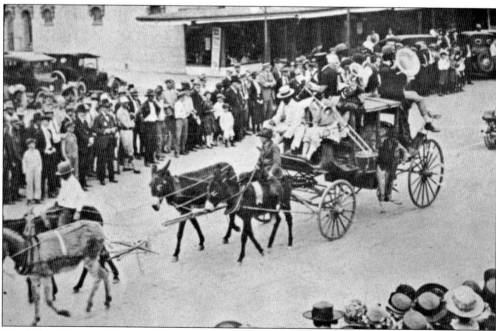

People loved to participate in parades. This one in downtown Abilene is from 1919, and donkeys are pulling a stagecoach with a small band on top. Much of history would have been lost if it was not for people photographing these early events.

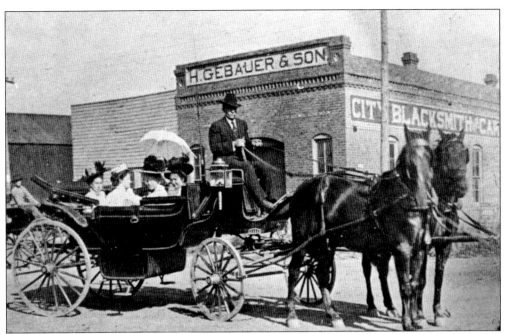

Parades were meant to show off different events or occasions. The "Queen of the City" and her ladies in waiting are being escorted in this 1910 parade. They are riding in a fine carriage pulled by a team of horses. It was quite an honor to be named the Queen of the City.

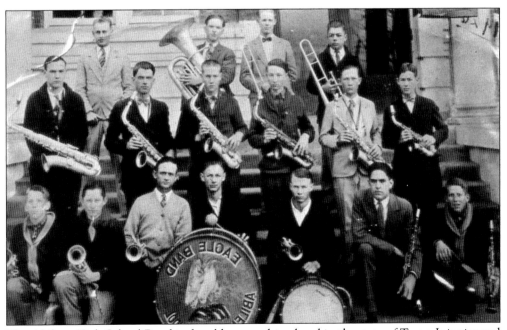

The Abilene High School Band is the oldest marching band in the state of Texas. It is pictured here in 1926, the first year it was formed. It performed not only for school events, but for civic events as well. The picture was taken on the steps of the city auditorium.

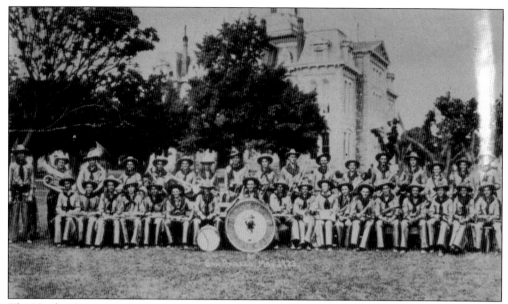

The Hardin-Simmons University Band was better known as the "Cowboy Band." The band today is known both nationally and internationally. The crowds love it when they do their famous "cowboy step" in parades. They are led by the school's famous six white horses.

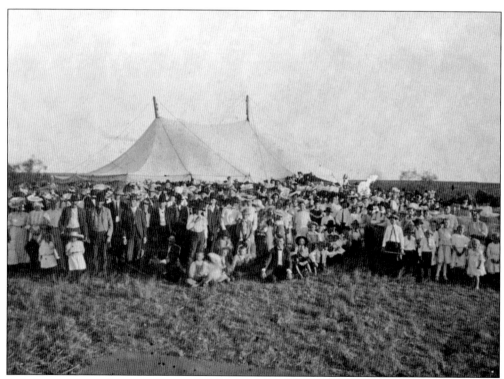

Religious tent revivals were well attended. Many of the churches were not yet built in early Abilene, so tent revivals were popular. Abilene was a wild and rough early Western town. People looked forward to getting a little religion whenever they could.

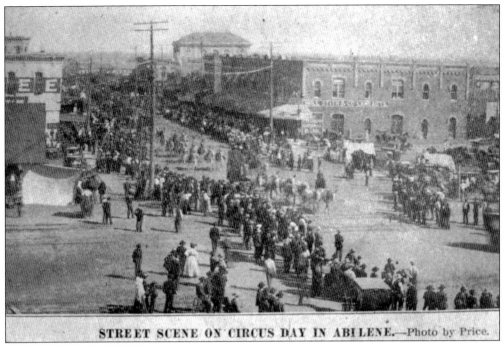

STREET SCENE ON CIRCUS DAY IN ABILENE.—Photo by Price.

A 1907 parade on Pine Street show that a circus has come to town, and the people turned out to watch the circus parade. Circuses moved around the country as they do today, and a parade announced their arrival in town. The kids almost dragged their parents downtown to watch.

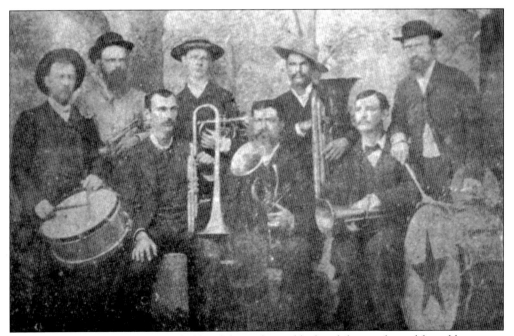

The Music Makers of 1885 was probably Abilene's first public band that performed for public events. Each member had some musical background, and so they came together to form this band.

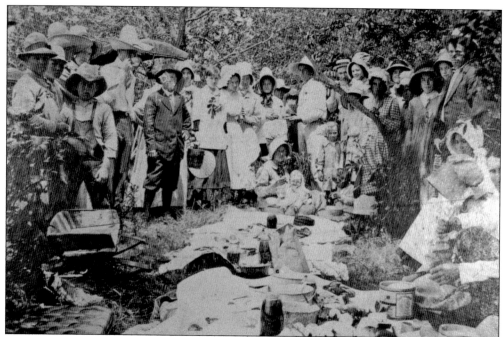

Picnics were another popular form of entertainment in early Abilene. A picnic gave families a chance to get out in the country and enjoy food and fellowship with their neighbors and friends. Note the clothing people wore on early picnics.

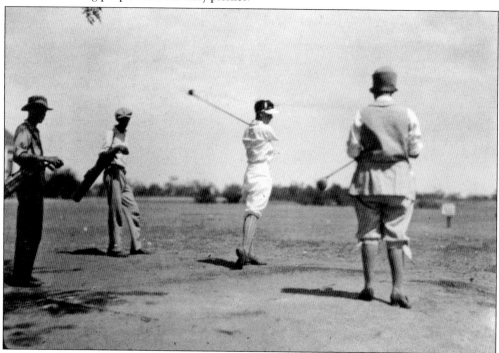

When golfing arrived in Abilene, people enjoyed a new sport that had not been available before. Women took up the sport as well. Caddies were very popular in the early days before golf carts arrived on the scene. There were soon private and public golf courses in the town.

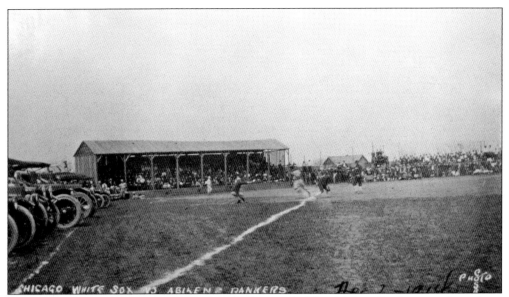

Baseball was another sport that arrived in Abilene early. The Abilene Bankers are shown here playing the Chicago White Sox. The Chicago team would stop along the route to play local teams when they were traveling home from spring training. Large crowds would turn out for these games.

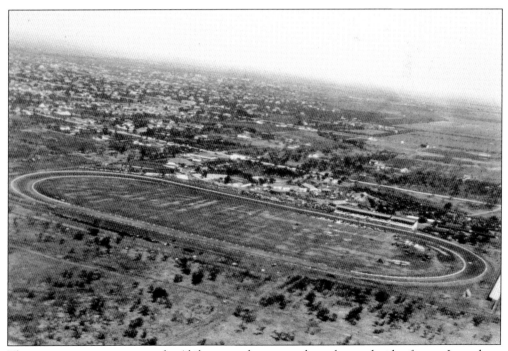

The main entertainment area for Abilene was the racetrack on the south side of town. It was here that all the races were held and the annual fair was held. Polo matches were held in the center of the track. Horses, motorcycles, and buggies were raced there at the track.

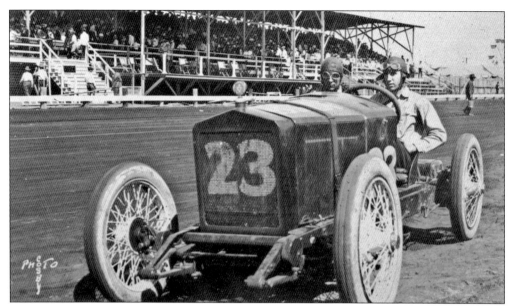

This racecar was typical of the automobiles that participated at Fair Park Race Track. Horses, buggies, dogs, and cars were raced at the track. Race day always brought out large crowds. The West Texas Fair was held at Fair Park for several decades, too.

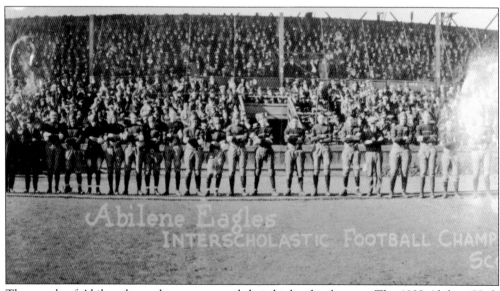

The people of Abilene have always supported their high school teams. The 1922 Abilene High School football team won the state championship game. The town had a big celebration and honored the members of that team.

Four

Early Abilene Churches and Schools

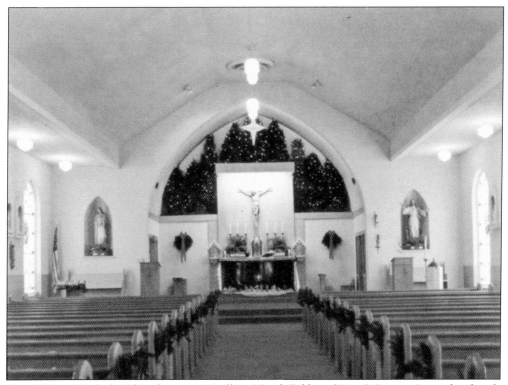

Sacred Heart Catholic Church was originally at North Fifth and Beech Streets. Later the church moved to South Eighth and Jeanette Streets, where it is located today. Abilene has always had a Catholic population and now has four Catholic churches.

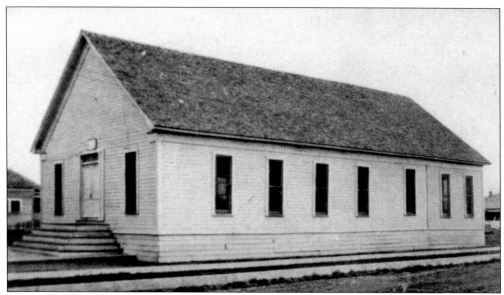

This is the Southside Church of Christ, located in Abilene. The Church of Christ has several churches in Abilene. Churches were well represented in the town. There is a Church of Christ University located there as well.

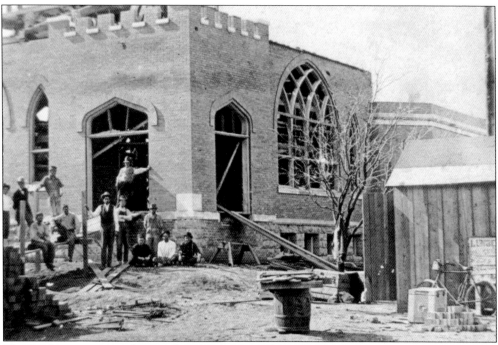

The Presbyterians were the very first congregation formed in Abilene. The early congregations met in members' homes and businesses. The Presbyterians built this church at North Second and Beech Streets. Now they are located at North Fifth and Orange Streets.

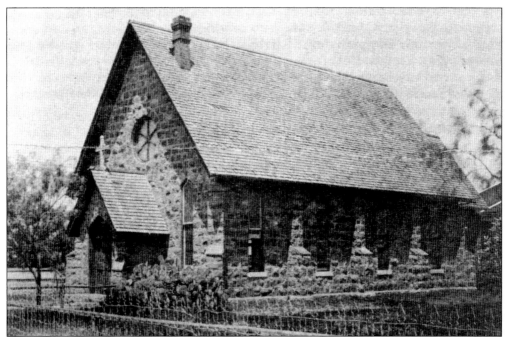

The Episcopal church was located at North Third and Orange Streets. This small church served its congregation well until a much larger church was built at South Sixth and Meander Streets. The site on Orange Street is currently where the First Baptist Church sanctuary is located.

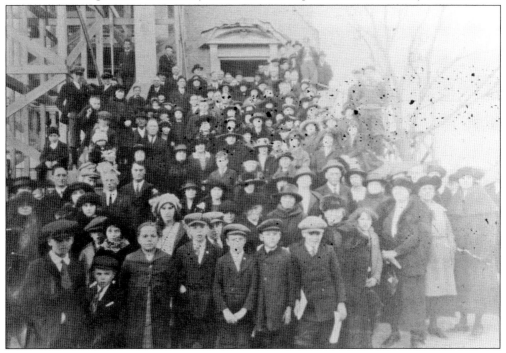

The congregation of the First Christian Church poses for a picture during the construction of their church at North Third and Orange Streets. This sanctuary served until a new one was built at the same location.

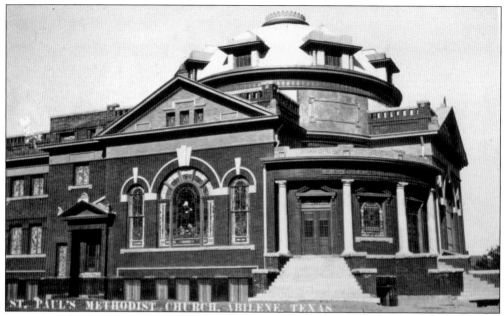

St. Paul Methodist Church was located at North Fifth and Beech Streets. The dome architect design was common to Methodist churches at the time. The congregation built a larger church across the street where the Sacred Heart Catholic Church used to be.

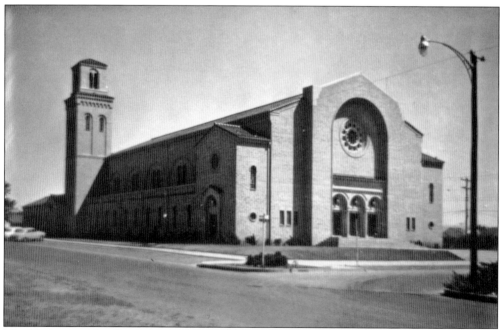

The University Church of Christ served its congregation and the students of Abilene Christian College from its location at North Sixteenth and Campus Court Streets. The church was recently enlarged at the same location.

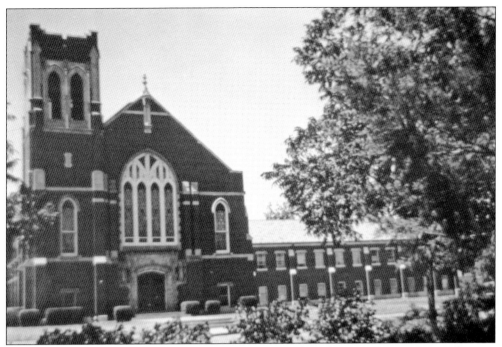

The First Presbyterian Church was located at North Fourth and Orange Streets. Later it became the First Central Presbyterian Church when two congregations joined together. A new sanctuary was built on the opposite end of the street.

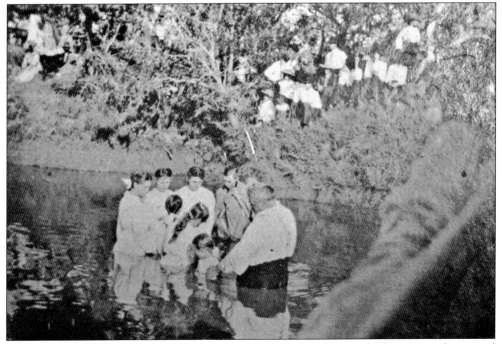

Before churches had baptisms in their sanctuaries, most baptisms took place in creeks around Abilene. These baptisms played an important part in church life and were well attended by their congregations.

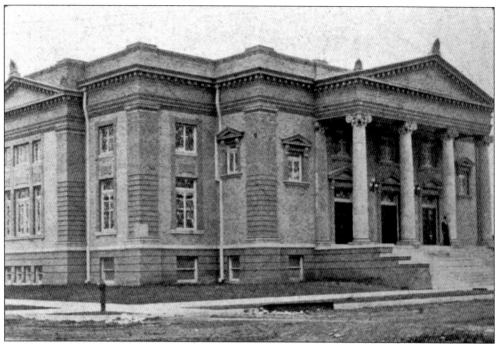

The First Baptist Church was located at North Second and Hickory Streets for several decades. Later a much larger sanctuary was built on the opposite corner, at North Third and Orange Streets. This sanctuary was torn down, and new wings were added to the church.

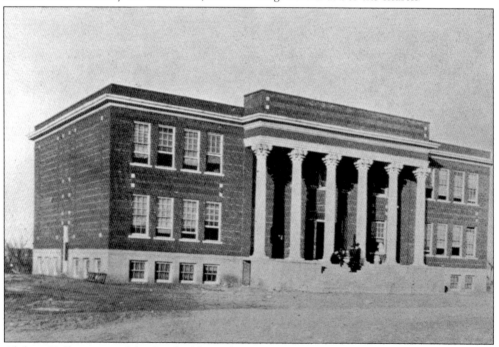

Abilene Hall was one of the first buildings that went up at the West Texas Baptist College. The university today is known as Hardin-Simmons University. It has always been located at Hickory Street and Ambler Street.

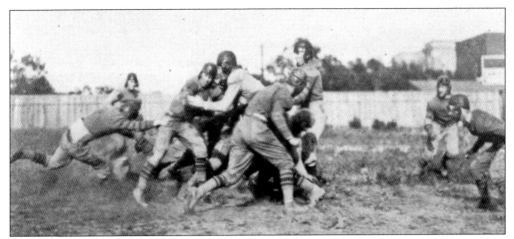

The game of football in 1922 was a rough and stressful game. Hardin-Simmons was one of the first football teams in this area. Members of these football teams were dedicated athletes, and they played in all kinds of weather for their schools.

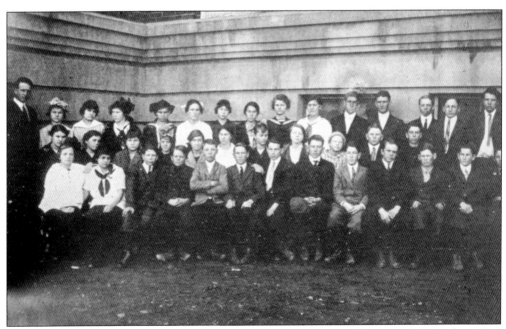

This group of young students represented the Corral Society of Abilene High School in 1914. The school was located at South Third and Peach Streets. Note the clothes that students wore for pictures in 1914. A new high school was later built at South First and Peach Streets.

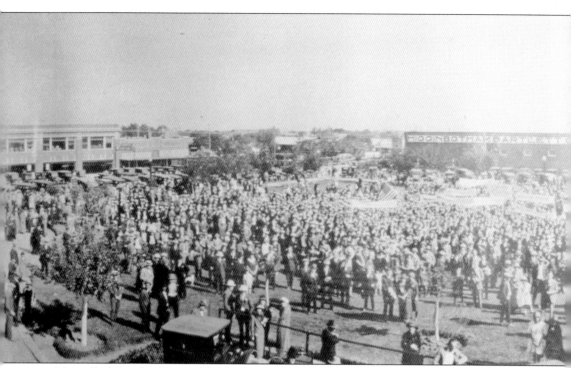

Most all of the churches in Abilene were represented at a meeting at the downtown bandstand in the early 1920s. It is not known what the occasion was, but a large crowd turned out for the citywide event. It was the custom in those days to support such events. Ministers hoped to pull the congregations together to endorse and support Christian projects.

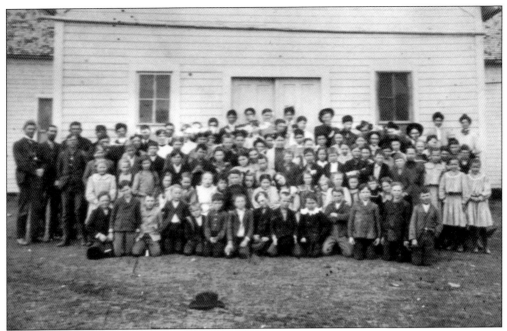

Border's Chapel School was typical of rural schools in this pre-1900 picture. Some rural schools had higher enrollments then others. Border's Chapel enjoyed a high enrollment of students. It was located near Abilene.

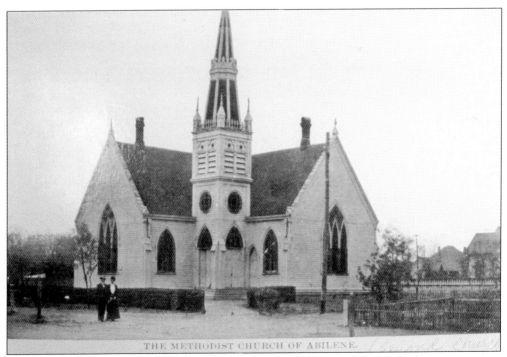

The Second Methodist Church is shown here in the pre-1900 picture. The Methodist congregations played an important role, as did the other congregations in Abilene, in taming the Wild West image of early Abilene.

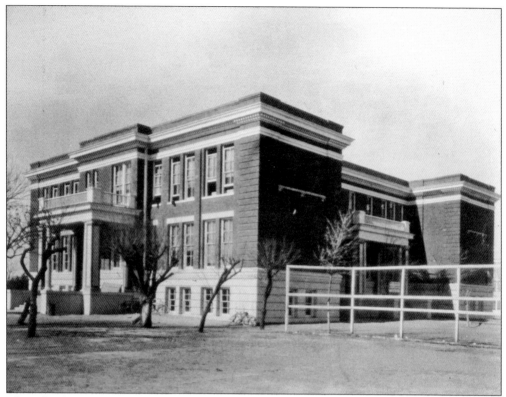

This school was constructed as the second high school in Abilene. Then it became a junior high school, and finally, it became known as Central Elementary School. It lasted as an elementary school until it was torn down in the 1960s.

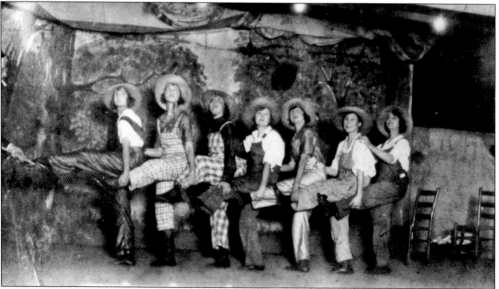

Schoolteachers entertained their students as they do today. The event is not named, but the teachers had a good time putting on a show for their students and parents. School was not all reading and arithmetic back in the early days.

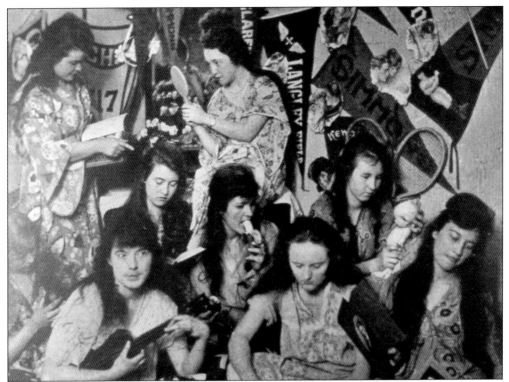

Girls at Simmons College having a dorm party in 1919. Dorm parties were one way female students could enjoy the college way of life.

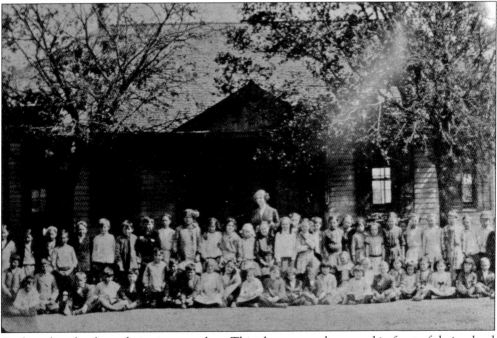

Students loved to have their pictures taken. This elementary class posed in front of their school with their teacher. Note the clothes that the children wore to school at the time of this image.

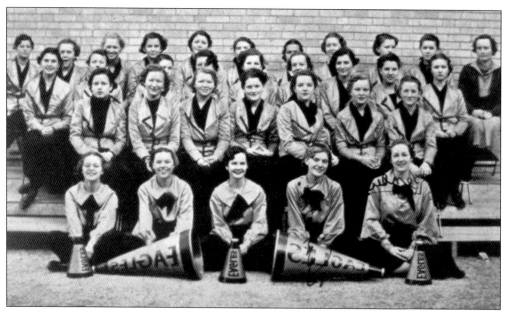

Abilene High School had its own prep squad in 1922. These girls supported Abilene High School athletic programs. The school colors have always been black and gold, but their costumes have evolved over the years.

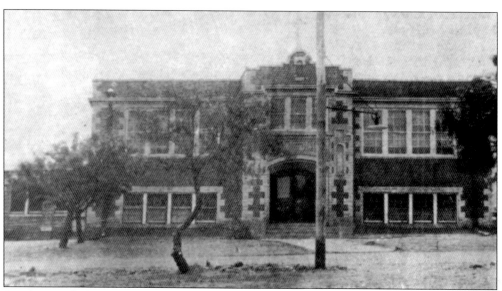

St. John's Catholic School was located on South Ninth Street. This Catholic school taught several grades and was operated by the Catholic Church. The nuns were the teachers and counselors for the students.

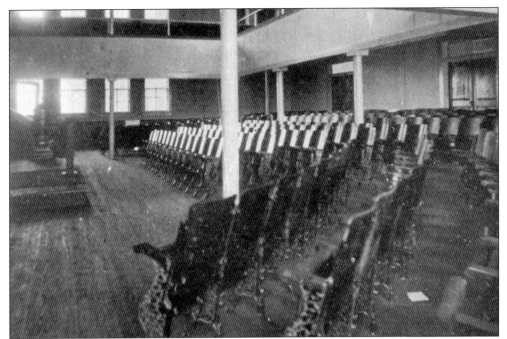

Childer's Classical Institute was located on North First Street. This picture shows the auditorium at the school. Later the school moved to the northeast part of town and was renamed Abilene Christian College. Today it is called Abilene Christian University.

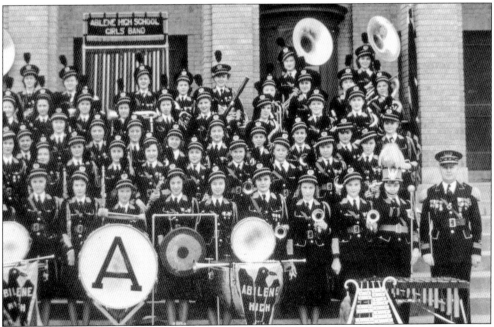

Besides having the oldest high school marching band in Texas, Abilene High School had one of the first all-girl bands in Texas. Their director Raymond Bynum was Abilene's longest-standing band director. He directed bands from the elementary through the college level and was known throughout the state.

www.arcadiapublishing.com

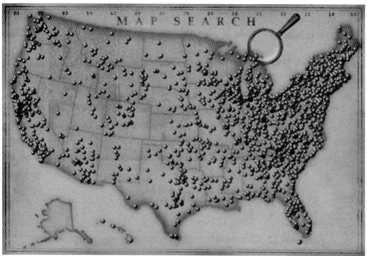

Discover books about the town where you grew up, the cities where your friends and families live, the town where your parents met, or even that retirement spot you've been dreaming about. Our Web site provides history lovers with exclusive deals, advanced notification about new titles, e-mail alerts of author events, and much more.

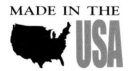

MADE IN THE USA

Arcadia Publishing, the leading local history publisher in the United States, is committed to making history accessible and meaningful through publishing books that celebrate and preserve the heritage of America's people and places. Consistent with our mission to preserve history on a local level, this book was printed in South Carolina on American-made paper and manufactured entirely in the United States.

This book carries the accredited Forest Stewardship Council (FSC) label and is printed on 100 percent FSC-certified paper. Products carrying the FSC label are independently certified to assure consumers that they come from forests that are managed to meet the social, economic, and ecological needs of present and future generations.

FSC
Mixed Sources
Product group from well-managed forests and other controlled sources

Cert no. SW-COC-001530
www.fsc.org
© 1996 Forest Stewardship Council

Find Your Place in History.